DOG EAT DOG

A VERY HUMAN BOOK
ABOUT DOGS AND DOG SHOWS

JANE AND MICHAEL STERN

SCRIBNER

SCRIBNER
1230 Avenue of the Americas
New York, NY 10020

DESIGNED BY ERICH HOBBING

Set in Garamond No. 3

Manufactured in the United States of America

1   3   5   7   9   10   8   6   4   2

Library of Congress Cataloging-in-Publication Data is available.

Stern, Jane
Dog eat dog: a very human book about dogs and dog shows/Jane and Michael Stern.
p.   cm.
1. Dog shows—United States—Anecdotes. 2. Show dogs—United States—Anecdotes. 3.
Dogs—Showing—Anecdotes. 4. Dog owners—United States—Anecdotes. 5. Einstein,
Mimi. I. Stern, Michael, date. II. Title.
SF425.15.S74   1997
636.7'0811—dc20   96–47055 CIP

ISBN 0-684-82253-9

Unless otherwise noted, all photos used in the photo section were taken by Michael Stern.

Acknowledgments

What pleasure it has been to write a book in the company of good dogs and the people who care for them. No expression of gratitude is sufficient to acknowledge the contribution of Mimi Einstein, who allowed us to trail her in and out of the show ring for more than a year, and whose love of all creatures is a joy to know. We also thank Jane Hobson, in whom we were privileged to see the skills and passion of a top competitor. In the homes of Ken and Debbie Vargas and Bill and Bonnie Wilson we came to know the devotion of earnest breeders engaged in work they love. Catharine Reiley was kind enough to share her tremendous knowledge of obedience work and of Poodles. Sam Kohl gave us a grand tour of his New York School of Dog Grooming. Jeanine O'Kane of the American Kennel Club provided vital statistics. Carol Beans, editor of *The Bullseye,* was kind enough to let us reprint her recipe for Twin Ham Roll-ups.

To Jim and Judy Monteith of Kimblewick Kennels we owe an incalculable debt of gratitude, for it was they who introduced us to Bullmastiffs many years ago. We are also much obliged to so many members of the American Bullmastiff Association who have tolerated our nosy ringside presence for so long.

We have been able to travel on the dog show circuit only because we can count on the able help of Bunny MacMannis

Acknowledgments

and Jean Wagner, who tend our own beloved animals when we are away.

Thanks, as usual, to Binky Urban for agenting with the ardor of a hilltopping hound. And our deep appreciation goes to editor Susan Moldow, whose belief in us, and in dogs, has been a constant motivation. We are also grateful to David Roth-Ey for his vigilant and enthusiastic assistance from the beginning.

Finally, we thank our two canine muses, Minerva and Clementine, who will never see a show ring but who are beautiful champions in our eyes.

—JANE & MICHAEL STERN

Contents

Introduction   11

1. Dog Show   17

2. Allstar Bullmastiffs   31

3. How a Dog Show Works   43

4. A Blue Ribbon in the Land of Pink and Green   51

5. When Poodles Reigned   67

6. Dog Days   73

7. Bizarre Breeds   81

8. Rusty Goes to Texas (The Dallas Specialty)   91

9. Showdown in Plano (Best of Breed)   103

10. Leonberger Love Connection   117

11. Rusty Come Home   125

12. Motherhood   135

13. The Dark Horse   147

14. The Beauty of the Beast   155

15. Madison Square Garden   163

16. Epilogue   181

Appendixes

1. Basic Show Dog Terms   185

2. Breeds Recognized by the AKC   187

3. The Most Popular Breeds   191

DOG EAT DOG

Introduction

There are twenty million purebred dogs in America; some two million of them compete against one another each year in contests sanctioned by the American Kennel Club. The sport of showing dogs has become a national pastime; and breeding them is a big business. The annual Westminster Kennel Club show at Madison Square Garden—the Superbowl of dogdom—is televised with star-studded black-tie hoopla like the presentation of the Academy Awards.

Dog shows were originally devised by bluebloods in England in the mid-nineteenth century, and for many years they remained a canine reflection of snob appeal. The American Kennel Club, founded in 1884, adopted a charter in 1909 mandating "the maintenance of the purity of thoroughbred dogs," a goal of little interest to most ordinary people who, if they had any kind of dog, probably had a mutt.

In the years after World War II a sea change in attitudes took place. For many Americans, owning a purebred dog became a perquisite of the good life. AKC registrations jumped from 77,400 in 1944 to 235,978 in 1949; the number of dog shows rose from a few hundred annually during the Truman era to the eleven thousand now sanctioned each year by the AKC.

We have become a nation of canine connoisseurs. Breeds that not long ago were extremely rare, such as the Shar-Pei, Akita, and Lhasa Apso, are now familiar sights in towns and cities everywhere; and many families once content to have a no-account mixed breed now scour stud books and seek out blood-lines of their dream Labrador, Rottweiler, or Siberian Husky.

It is not uncommon for many people who acquire a pedigreed dog to want to show it. We did. As newlyweds twenty-five years ago we scraped together some cash and bought a puppy. Some couples dream of a house, others of a baby; we could think of nothing more enriching to our tender relationship than the companionship of a drooling, flatulent Bulldog.

Richard was a purebred. He came with a pedigree, a family tree of dogs with flamboyant names and titles far more grand than anything in our own lineage. Richard soon became the centerpiece of our lives. We spent days admiring this beautiful animal and looking time and again at his ancestral papers. It wasn't long before it occurred to us that it was only fair to share his magnificence with the world.

We were certain that because he was the most beautiful dog on earth, he would inspire awe at any dog show. Through the local Bulldog club, we learned about a small show nearby. We were advised by a member of the club to enter Richard in a Sweepstakes class. That term meant nothing to us, but it sounded sufficiently grand, conjuring up notions of the Irish Sweepstakes. We were soon disappointed to learn that Sweepstakes is for young dogs, most of whom have little previous experience in the show ring.

That first dog show was—to put it kindly—a learning experience. Before the day was over, our precious Richard had gone from being the benchmark of everything a dog should be to a washout. Why was it that we never noticed the funny shape of his head, or the way his hind legs angled out, or the waddle in his walk? The judge gave him only a cursory look, asking us kindly if he had ever been shown before, a question no doubt prompted when Richard rolled on his back in the grass as he was supposed to be standing for inspection, then wildly pulled on the judge's trouser cuffs when the judge tried to walk away.

For the rest of the day we sat on the sidelines of the show and watched the action. We realized that even this little event was part of a special world—a subculture with its own rules, lingo, and codes of behavior. The world of dog shows is based on a love of dogs and a desire to produce beautiful examples of a breed, but it has little to do with the simple and time-honored emotional bond that defines the relationship of a pet and its master.

Although shows are open to anyone with a registered pure-bred, the chances of a novice taking a nice-looking dog into the ring and winning big in a significant show are about as good as sending your home video to the Academy of Motion Picture Arts and Sciences and picking up an Oscar for it. Dog shows exist to recognize breed perfection, but they also reward those men and women who devote lifetimes to the service of showing and breeding. And like Hollywood, book publishing, or just about any big business, the world of dog shows is highly political: Big advertising campaigns in trade papers and tons of money spent campaigning top dogs have an undeniable, although unquantifiable, influence on who takes home the trophy.

The life of most professional show dogs is not much like the life led by an ordinary pet. Some lucky ones do spend time at home, romping in the backyard and lounging on a cushion in the den; but the heavy hitters can't afford to be away from the ring for too long. Like cowboys who rodeo for a living, top show dogs spend most of the year on the road, living out of vans and motel rooms, traveling to wherever the stakes are highest.

Introduction

Breeders and handlers who take animals on the circuit need a different attitude from those of us who think the sun rises and sets on our Fluffies, Fidos, and Foo-foos. In addition to deep pockets, those who show on a regular basis must maintain an unsentimental eye. They may love their animals very much, but they need to look at them the way a poker player sizes up a hand. However fine you think your dogs are, if you plan to show them, you need to be a supreme strategist. Who is judging a particular show? What are this season's breed trends? Which dogs are yours up against? To be consistently successful in this competitive world, breeders and handlers must know all the tricks to make a mediocre dog look great, and to make a great dog maintain an edge. Most of all, they need to want to win so badly that their bones ache for it.

It is their world that is the focus of our book.

To explore dog shows, we chose one person as our main guide. We needed someone who would allow us unlimited access to what can be a secretive world. We wanted a veteran in the game who was somewhere between an amateur who goes to shows on summer Sundays for a lark and the wealthy elite who hire people to take their dogs around the country from show to show in private jets, and who spend hundreds of thousands of dollars each year earning blue ribbons, but who aren't personally involved in the day to day travails of the show ring.

Mimi Einstein perfectly filled the bill.

Mimi, who runs Allstar Kennel in Katonah, New York, is a well-respected, long-time player in the dog show game. Allstar has produced top-winning champion Bullmastiffs for nearly two decades; Mimi's walls are garlanded with ribbons they have won and her tables are heavy with silver loving cups. Her credentials as an animal person go beyond the dog show world: She is president of the Westchester Society for the Prevention of Cruelty to Animals, where in addition to running the business end of things she is also an officer who personally goes out on animal abuse and rescue cases. She is the founder of Golden Outreach, a program developed to promote the use of dogs in therapy for disabled and mentally challenged people. She has participated in Pegasus, a horseback riding program for handicapped children. And she serves on the board of directors of the American Bullmastiff Association, which has selected her to judge at its 1997 National Specialty Show. The specialty show is the top venue for the breed, but because Mimi is judging it this year, none of her own dogs can be entered—a sacrifice for a serious breeder, but a supreme honor for someone who deeply cares about her breed.

Mimi became our focus also because she is utterly authentic, which is the greatest gift a writer can receive. She allowed us to share her involvement in the world of showing and breeding with no limitations and no pretense. Her professional joys and triumphs were as unvarnished as her rivalries and occasional ill will. As she led us through a year on the circuit, she never once pulled a punch or sugarcoated the sometimes stormy politics of the game. Through it all, we saw a story based on an underlying love for dogs and a missionary zeal to produce the best of a breed.

And, oh, yes: it didn't hurt that Mimi breeds our favorite kind of dog, the Bullmastiff. She is also the only person we can think of with the chutzpah to walk into Mike Tyson's house and take back the dog she sold him. But you'll read about that later on.

Because Mimi lives in New York State, her dogs are mostly shown in the Northeast. There are dog shows all over the country, for that matter all over the world; but it is her world, that of the shows, breeders, handlers, and judges of the East Coast on which this book is focused. But we believe her story is universal. Her goals are those of breeders everywhere whom we met while researching this book. She wants to produce beautiful dogs that are her ideal vision of the breed standard. She loves the dogs she produces; she spends far more money than she makes breeding them; and there are times when the sheer frustrations of the show ring and the whelping pen make her want to pack it all in. But for many years now, she has not; and we doubt she ever will.

Why did she want us to tell her story? Our best guess is that like other top breeders, she wants the public to see how difficult it is to do the job right. Mimi knows firsthand that the ever-increasing popularity of purebreds and dog shows means that more people want to get into breeding and showing; yet many who have this ambition are clueless about all that it requires. The popular notion that you can go to the local pet shop, buy a male and a female registered something-or-other, let them mate, then sell the puppies for a fortune would be laughable if it weren't also often tragic. The breeding and showing of purebred dogs is a serious business best done for love, not easy money, because it is an obstacle course fraught with disaster and heartbreak; and it can be bank-busting costly, too.

We have interspersed Mimi's show year diary with vignettes of others we met along the circuit. You will meet people who breed dogs designed to kill, dogs that are hairless and look like polka-dotted martians, men and women who groom poodles for a living and will dye them shocking pink for a small extra charge, and a pair of first-time breeders who strive to do everything with utter perfection. You will also meet one of our favorite characters, a man who loves dogs so much he cannot bring himself to buy one.

Dog shows are a funny world. We hope you enjoy the trip.

CHAPTER 1

Dog Show

Sunday, May 7 is a deliriously beautiful day at Mercer County Park, near Princeton, New Jersey, where the Trenton Kennel Club holds its sixty-sixth annual all-breed show. The spring air is crisp; stiff wind flaps the canvas on the blue and gold striped tents adjacent to grass show rings under a cloudless sky. The setting would be perfect for a carefree picnic, but what is about to take place is a dog fight—one of the first skirmishes of the season in an ongoing war among purebred canines to determine which among them are the best. Dogs are the soldiers in these battles, but tactics are planned and strategy is charted by human beings: breeders and breed loyalists, handlers and groomers. Some dogs enjoy themselves in the show ring, others do not; but all the people who put them there relish the competition. Like gamblers in a floating poker game, they travel from show to show almost every weekend so they and their dogs can best their rivals.

More than three thousand dogs, from Affenpinschers to Yorkshire Terriers, and from pocket-size Papillons to eye-level Irish Wolfhounds have been brought to Princeton today to compete with one another. They are scheduled to be shown in twenty-five different rings from 8:30 in the morning to late in the afternoon, when they will be judged by people certified by the American Kennel Club, which sanctions the show. Although credit is given to a contender for attitude (a Doberman should be watchful and alert; a terrier must appear high-spirited; a Bulldog has to seem stalwart), intelligence or goodness for its own sake is not a major asset of a show dog. And while talent is prized by some pet owners and by all who use dogs to hunt, herd cattle, lead the sightless and the deaf, rescue disaster victims, sniff drugs or bombs, or police the streets, it matters little in the show ring. In fact, there are many other kinds of canine contests that test animals' vocational skills. But when most people think of a dog show, they think of one like that staged by the Trenton Kennel Club: a "conformation show," meaning that the single fundamental quality that makes a winner is bodily perfection.

This event at Mercer County Park is the second of a quartet of shows held over the course of one long weekend in early May each year around Philadelphia. It is preceded by the Bucks County Kennel Club Show and followed by shows in Harmony and Newton, New Jersey. The four-day circuit is known informally among dog people as the "East Coast Weekend"; it marks the beginning of the region's outdoor summer season, and if you have a dog you want to make a champion, this is where the campaign must start. Victories won during the East Coast Weekend foretell greatness.

At dawn in the park, squadrons of vehicles are encamped around the perimeter, many of them showing their allegiance to a favorite breed with bumper stickers that announce I ♥ BULLDOGS or WARNING: ROTTWEILER ON BOARD. License plates are another way to announce fealty: VISZLA1, HOTROTS, GDANES, PCORGI, and one that simply says WOOOF. Vans and full-size motor homes are the preferred form of transportation for many professional handlers and owner/handlers who spend the year on the dog show circuit. The big vehicles permit occupants to be more self-reliant. They are a way to avoid the indignity and expense of trying to check into a motel with a pack of dogs as your companions.

It is not unusual for small-timers to exhibit some jealousy toward the motor home occupants. This morning in Princeton, the issue is toilet paper. Contestants lined up at the Port-O-Sans are accusing them of taking it all. Emerging from a paperless portable toilet, a large woman in a tight DANDIE DINMONTS DO IT IN THE DIRT sweatshirt rages about the temerity of the motor home crowd. "They drive here in their hundred-thousand-dollar vehicles, then they steal our toilet paper!" she fumes as others waiting in line growl with righteous indignation. "They live like millionaires, but they cannot buy their own damn Charmin."

For a big show like this, many contestants arrive and take positions around the field the night before. They set up their living quarters, chat with neighbors and share recent show results, and plan strategy with groomers and handlers. Before the break of day, they begin preparing their dogs. Some animals require as much as four hours' grooming before entering the ring: bathing, combing, clipping, braiding; applications of powder and perfume. Even those that aren't so magnificently coiffured need to be cleaned; and more important, the handlers need to hone their dogs' psychological edge so they can present their best qualities to utmost advantage in the ring. For each breed, that requires a different kind of preparation. In the wide open spaces at the edge of the park, sporting dogs go jogging with their handlers while terriers zig-zag through the grass inhaling delicious scents. An energetic Labrador retriever chases a Frisbee thrown by his owner. A stately Mastiff sits on his haunches, watching other playful dogs from the sidelines, getting into his own properly vigilant frame of mind.

Whatever your preferred breed, a dog show is the place to wallow in it. Not just looking at the show ring, but shopping. The dog fancy has generated a tremendous commercial subculture of products that range from practical to preposterous. Want to turn your "dog combings" into a lovely sweater? A company called Creature Comforts out of Vashon, Washington, will make yarn or whole blankets from the fur you send them. "Piddle pants" offer a practical solution to incontinence in puppies and elderly dogs. Dog Master Systems promises "near hypnotic control" of any dog by using a set of sound-makers that you squeeze in the palm of your hand. Lazy owners of active dogs will be happy to know about the Dog-A-Polt, a "self-launched retrieving toy." Sybaritic animals will appreciate Woods Waterbeds for pets. And city folks who want to leave the sidewalk clean no longer need carry bowel movements away in little lunch bags if they get the the Dignifido Collar Pak Dog Waste System for carrying picked-up stools in a pouch around the neck of the dog who made them. There are pet car seats, "pet pouches" for transporting little Fido like a baby kangaroo, Pet Saver Totes to sling over the shoulder when climbing down a fire escape, and, of course, high-quality ceramic urns for a favorite pet's "cremains."

Marion Krups, a Scottie enthusiast, has taken a break from her retail booth where she and her husband sell dog-related fine art. She strolls around the grounds and runs into two friends she saw last at a meeting of the Wee Scots, an Indiana-based social club for people who like Scotties and collect Scottie memorabilia. After exchanging pleasantries about the weather, she strolls on, calling back to them to come see her at her booth. "Come visit us. We're right next to the cooked liver," she says with a wave, referring to the booth where cooked and dried meat is sold for handlers to perk their dogs' interest in the ring.

Even though the sky is blazingly blue and it is T-shirt weather, Randall, a Chinese Crested dog, is shivering outside of ring 21, where he is scheduled to be judged at 9:50 A.M. It is no wonder he is cold: except for a leonine tuft of hair on the top of his head, and a few fluffs from the knees down, Randall is hairless. He is sitting on his owner Lee Bakuckas's lap as she rubs his bare skin with Nivea cream and fluffs his mane with a comb. Randall, whose show name is Champion Lejo's Les Toreadores and is out of Champion Razzmatazz Cashmeri Lejo by Champion Eric's Crescentmoon Omen of Oz, scarcely weighs more than his pedigree. He is a spectacularly weird-looking creature. His naked skin is bright pink with big mauve polka dots that make him look like something Dr. Doolittle created on a whim, and he is smaller than a house cat. A handful of gawkers gather to watch Randall being groomed. "I believe in using people products on hairless dogs," Mrs. Bakuckas lectures to the crowd. "Randall's skin is very special. In the winter, if it isn't well taken care of, you see a lot of problems: zits and dry flaky skin. In the summer, he tans and looks better." Mrs. Bakuckas is thrilled to be telling people about a passion she has had since long before the American Kennel Club even recognized Chinese Crested dogs as a breed. "When I got my first Crested fifteen years ago, I was the only person in Pennsylvania who had one," she says. "Back then, they were considered freaks."

When she has finished rubbing the shivering Randall down with moisturizer she holds him aloft triumphantly and lets the group of people gathered around admire the smoothness of his skin and the silky texture of his hair. She explains that because it looks naked, the Chinese Crested dog was once favored as a pet by strip-tease artists. Gypsy Rose Lee was among the first people to promote the breed. "She so enjoyed posing with them that heads of state would run out and get a hairless dog just so they could have their picture taken with her," Mrs. Bakuckas reveals. "Of course, they aren't Chinese at all. They were originally African. But Chinese merchants took them aboard ship and used them as ratters. Then when all the rats were eaten, they would eat the dog. They were a larger breed then."

Looking at tiny, trembling, polka-dotted Randall, it is hard to imagine him providing much of a meal for a hungry sailor. "I always keep my home at seventy-two degrees," Mrs. Bakuckas tells the awestruck crowd. "That way I don't have to put any clothing on him."

Randall the Chinese Crested dog is not the only one at the show suffering from the brisk May air. The breezes create major problems in the grooming tents where dogs that require significant cosmetological attention are positioned atop portable tables and attended by their beauticians. From large Standard Poodles to tiny Shih Tzus, they perch patiently as they are gone over with brushes, combs, electric hair dryers, and profuse amounts of hair spray. But because the tents have open sides, the wind whips through the aisles, mussing fur and contaminating gleaming coats with dust. Groomers use hair nets, shower caps, scrunchies, and rubber bands to try to protect their beauties from the elements right up until show time, but one commentator compares the experience to keeping a neat hairdo while enduring "desert-type wind storms."

Bullmastiffs and their owners, on the other hand, enjoy the bracing breeze. The big, short-coated dogs have unmussable fur and plenty of flesh to keep them warm. They even have inherent facial makeup in the form of black masks and kohl-like eye shadow that requires no extra grooming artifice. They are a breed shown pretty much au naturel, the only special beautician's tool required being a towel so that ropes of drool can be wiped from their juicy flews just before the judge inspects them. Handlers call the towel a slop rag, and around ring 11, where the Bullmastiffs are to be judged at 11:15, nearly half the people gathered have one tucked into their belt or waistband. Newfoundlands have been in ring 11 since 10:15, and before them came Beagles, Norwegian Elkhounds, Rhodesian Ridgebacks, and Standard Schnauzers.

About 10:30, nearly an hour before they are to be judged, the Bullmastiffs start appearing around the outside of the ring. Tension begins to grow as handlers and owners eye the arriving competition and Bullmastiffs sniff air that is luscious with the scent of dogs and bitches in their prime. The Bullmastiff fancy, like that of most breeds, is a small world; those on the show circuit know and compete against one another regularly; and the champion dogs entered in the Best of Breed class have reputations that precede them. But the marshaled contestants, human and canine, cannot help but get excited by the drama about to transpire on this first big weekend of the show year in the East. Among today's entries is a big four-year-old Bullmastiff male named Allstar's Play It Again Sam, who two years earlier took blue ribbons back-to-back at Bucks County and Trenton—a remarkable triumph that made Sam appear to be unstoppable. But suddenly he disappeared from the show circuit. Now he is back, and if his old magic can be rekindled, he will be the dog to beat this weekend and for the rest of the season.

Sired by one of the great modern studs, Champion Allstar's Terry Thomas, out of Bravo's Rhapsody in Red, Allstar's Play It Again Sam is what Bullmastiff people call a "typey" dog, meaning he shows all the characteristics of the breed to maximum effect. He was on his way to greatness two years back, but after his Trenton victory, Sam accidentally tore a ligament in a hind leg. Two surgeries rendered him gimpy for a year. Time and pampered rest at home finally brought him back to soundness. At four years old—late in life to re-enter the competitive fray—his owner's mission is to earn his championship and rack up enough big wins to firmly establish him as the reigning standard of Bullmastiff beauty.

Sam is exquisite. He is a one-hundred-fifty-pound brick of brawn with a broad, well-padded head set on a thirty-four-inch neck sturdy as oak. His short muzzle is black, and at the top of this inky mask, two mahogany brown eyes peer out below a thick, simian brow. The expression on his face is arresting—the imperturbable look of a sentry so formidable that his mere glance is enough to send scurrying away any would-be transgressor. His short-haired coat is brindle—a riot of brown and black tiger stripes that give him natural camouflage, especially at night, when only the gleam of his eyes and the flash of his ivory-white teeth might belie his presence in the darkness. Most Bullmastiffs today are solid shades of red or fawn (all have black masks), but Sam's dark stripes are closer to what the original developers of the breed had in mind a hundred years ago, in England, when they crossed the stately Mastiff with the pugnacious Bulldog. Their goal was to develop a working animal suited to prowling and protecting the estates of the landed gentry—as formidable as a Mastiff but more agile, and with the Bulldog's tenacity. The result was a new breed of dog that was fearless but not ferocious, that could sprint fast but throw enough bulk to knock down a big man, and that had the composure to keep an intruder at bay without tearing out his throat. Recognized by the Kennel Club of Great Britain in the 1920s and by the American Kennel Club a decade later, Bullmastiffs were originally known as "the game keeper's night dog"; all the qualities that once made them such good sentinels have now become the official breed standard, and are the measure by which Bullmastiffs are supposed to be judged.

As a show dog, Sam has a hard road back to the summit. Even if his bum leg is no longer a problem, he is middle-aged for a breed that rarely lives beyond eight or ten. The dog show ring, like human beauty pageants, mostly rewards youth: jaunty, eager dogs get blue ribbons. When Sam was two years old, he tore around the show rings of the East Coast Weekend full of fire. Now at age four, he stands nobly when the judge examines him and he dutifully gaits to and fro when he is asked, but there is no ignoring his blasé expression. *"I don't really care,"* Sam announces with a sigh when he launches into a circle around the show ring, trotting with the ponderous force of an Eisenhower-era Buick.

Sam has come to Trenton in the company of his owner and breeder, Mimi Einstein. A tall, slim woman in her mid-fifties with short dark hair and brown eyes, Mimi arrives at the show outfitted in a no-nonsense uniform of dark green sweatshirt, blue jeans, white sneakers, and dark sunglasses, leading Sam at the end of a leash held in one hand. In her other hand is a large metal water pail, which she puts on the grass near the Bullmastiff ring for Sam to drink from. He lowers his massive muzzle, laps away, and pulls back with ropes of saliva trailing from his chin. Mimi whips out her slop rag and swipes it back and forth in a brisk motion perfected by experience; and instantly Sam's foot-and-a-half jawspan is show-ring clean.

For the beginning of the season and the East Coast Weekend, Mimi Einstein has placed her hopes on three dogs from her Allstar Kennel. In addition to Sam, she is fielding a novice two-year-old bitch named Sugar and a two-year-old male named Rusty, who is already a champion of record. At Trenton, the second of the four shows, she is already in a bad mood. Bucks County, the day before, did not go well. Sugar, who had never been shown, circled halfway around the ring then stopped in her tracks, ignoring the judge so she could eyeball some dogs on the sidelines. Sam, Mimi's personal darling, plodded around in a state of supreme ennui. Rusty showed well and almost took the best of breed ribbon, but he was beaten out by another champion handled by veteran showman Alan Levine, a man with whom Mimi Einstein has a long-standing rivalry.

Levine, a top-ranked professional handler for forty years, is an eye-catching presence in his white straw Panama hat, seersucker sports jacket, and trademark white mustache waxed and turned up in baroque curlicues at the tips, with a reefer-thin cigar that he puffs while outside the ring measuring the competition. His iconography is that of a melodrama's villain, but in fact he is an avuncular character, at least out of the ring. His easy banter and his storehouse of jokes remind one more of an old-time traveling salesman who can charm any housewife into buying a new Fuller brush.

As the Bullmastiff owners and handlers congregate under the tent before the judging starts, Alan Levine walks past Mimi with the Bullmastiff he is currently handling, Champion Ladybug Thorn of the Rose B.D. He has been campaigning Thorn around the country for two years, and as the summer season begins, he has made him the top-winning Bullmastiff in the nation. He greets Mimi cordially and she returns the greeting. The dark glasses she wears barely conceal the sparks of competitive fire in her gaze.

She sizes up Levine's dog Thorn and as the breed judging approaches, she confers with her own handler Jane Hobson. When Mimi began showing dogs, she took them in the ring herself; but like most serious contenders, she soon realized the advantages of hiring a professional—someone who handles show dogs for a living, knows all the tricks of the trade, and, perhaps even more important, is known to all the judges. Jane has handled Mimi's dogs for the last five years, starting in 1990 when Allstar had so many dogs going into the ring at one time at the Westminster Kennel Club show in New York that Mimi found herself with more dogs to show than she could handle. At the time Jane had no high-powered reputation; but Mimi was desperate, so she handed Jane Allstar's Mae West to show in the Open Bitch class. Mae West took the blue ribbon, and Jane has shown Allstar dogs ever since. A pretty, slim-waisted, athletic woman in her mid-thirties with short, dark hair and a glittering line of about a half-dozen small diamond studs in the helix of her ear, Jane wears a simple flowery dress nipped at the waist, sneakers, and a team jacket that has the words EAST COAST SCHUTZHUND AND POLICE DOG CLUB embroidered on the back. In addition to handling Mimi's Bullmastiffs, Jane also handles Rottweilers in all-breed shows, like Trenton, as well as in schutzhund work, which consists of competitions that measure protection instinct and obedience skills. Before she goes into the ring, though, she removes the schutzhund jacket, keeping a large leather fanny pack strapped to her waist. This is her "bait bag," filled with tidbits of hot dogs, cooked liver, pork chops, boneless chicken, and pâté that she uses in the ring as a lure and as a reward to get the dog she is showing to perk up. Jane has her own secret recipe for cooking liver so it is dry enough to tear easily into bite-size pieces, yet still moist and succulent enough to make the dogs happy. To keep it handy when she is in the show ring, Jane stuffs huge pieces of it in her cheek, making her look like a baseball player with a wad of chewing tobacco. As needed, she reaches into her mouth and pulls out bits of the stuff to get the dog's attention when the judge looks her way. "I've got a five-course meal in here!" she boasts before leading Mimi's Sugar into the ring for the Open Bitch competition to see if the young dog can do better than her miserable debut at Bucks County the day before.

As Jane takes Sugar into the ring with the other bitches, Mimi repeats a whispered litany: "Please Sugar, Sugar, don't collapse." Sugar starts to tug against her leash, growing wild and uncontrolled, and Mimi squeezes her hands together in a kind of muscular prayer. "No, don't do that" she says to the air. Jane is pulling pieces of liver from her cheek at a rapid pace as the dogs complete their run in a circle and are then lined up in show stances. Jane has her under control for the moment that the judge, William Paul Shelton, comes to inspect her. Mr. Shelton is a ruddy young man with a pug nose who looks like he truly enjoys the parade of dogs displayed before him. After walking back and forth, then making the handlers strut around a few additional times, then arranging and rearranging the bitches to compare various specimens side by side, he puts Sugar at the head of the line and points to her as number one. A few moments later, when she competes against bitches from all the other classes, she once again goes to the head of the line. She is the Winner's Bitch, which means she garners five full points toward her championship. Mimi shrieks with joy and hugs her friends. In one miraculous event, Sugar has gone from goofy puppy to winning show dog.

But like a gambler on a roll, Mimi's satisfaction at the win quickly evaporates as she looks ahead to the next engagement in the ring: Best of Breed. Of the three dogs she brought today, Sam is already dead in the water, eliminated from the match in the Open Dog competition when he was betrayed by his boredom. But Sugar, being Winner's Bitch, and Rusty, already a champion, are both in the running, and the pair are a good hand to be holding as Best of Breed competition begins. Because Allstar's handler, Jane Hobson, cannot show two dogs at once, Mimi turns Sugar over to Alan Levine's assistant. Despite professional rivalries, it is a common practice for dog handlers to help one another in a pinch. But unlike Jane, Levine's assistant is unaware of how green Sugar is and is taken by surprise when the young bitch breaks stride while circling the ring and tries to head for the sidelines. Sensing she's got a patsy at the top of the leash, Sugar digs in her heels and refuses to move. "Let's go, Punky!" the handler says gamely.

"It's Sugar, her name is Sugar!" Mimi calls out, hoping to help, and miraculously, Sugar stops bucking and trots calmly around the ring. Still, she is too callow to show well against the poised and confident Thorn; and although Rusty shows well, he too eats Thorn's dust. When it's all over, Sugar and Rusty go home with Jane. Sam, of course, stays with Mimi.

Despite Sugar's first major win, Mimi walks away from Trenton disconsolate. Sam's loss is an emotional defeat; she likes him too much to take his defeat in stride, declaring "He is simply too good a dog for these judges, too much Bullmastiff for someone who doesn't know what they're looking at." She lights a cigarette, staring deeply into Sam's soulful eyes, which look back at her unblinking and serene. She cannot really blame him for preferring the easy life at home to parading around the show ring. With Sam in tow, she heads toward the edge of the park, where her red Astrovan contains his large wire travel crate.

She pulls away from the show, leaving behind the circuslike tents and the commotion of the crowds looking at dogs still working their way toward the climactic Best in Show competition. Refocusing her gaze in the rearview mirror, she can see Sam's broad head in his crate, his eyes bright and beaming her way. On the interstate highway as she looks for a Burger King where she can buy Sam a Whopper, and one for herself as well, her thoughts are on the next show down the line. His, no doubt, are on the couch back home.

CHAPTER 2

Allstar Bullmastiffs

Mimi Einstein has an old-fashioned one-armed bandit in her house that takes her quarters and sometimes gives them back to her when she hits the jackpot. When there is a dog show in eastern Connecticut, she finds time to work the slot machines at the Foxwoods Casino. And she admits to sometimes spending hours trying to beat her own home computer at poker when she knows she really ought to be working on more important projects for the Westchester Society for the Prevention of Cruelty to Animals. Mimi likes to gamble. She doesn't do it for big stakes, and she isn't addicted to it, but she is someone who delights in the thrill of the risk and the long-shot odds of winning big.

Dog shows appeal to her for the same reasons, and while she seldom wins at games of chance, she has had extraordinary success in the ring. You win no money at dog shows—just ribbons, trophies, and glory—but the competition that takes place over the course of a year offers all the intrigue and cunning of an ongoing game of seven-card stud with wild cards and jokers dealt when you least expect them. Like a coterie of professional gamblers, most of the opponents in the Bullmastiff ring form a kind of ad hoc family; there is affection and there are some strong loyalties among them, as well as a large measure of distrust, some fear and loathing, and a burning desire to trump one's rivals. Like poker, dog fancy is a game that requires both a large amount of skill and a good measure of luck, with some elements beyond your control (genetic flukes, dumb judges, your particular opponents on any given day) and other elements you can play like a card sharp with an ace up your sleeve. As a breeder of Bullmastiffs since the early 1980s, Mimi Einstein has shown great talent and has had good luck in her ability to develop a distinctive bloodline; and she has become one of the top players in the breed.

Mimi has always loved animals. First there were horses, on which she competed in hunter-jumper classes as a girl, then as a young woman. Framed photographs around the house show her as a sleek teenager with a striking resemblance to Isabella Rossellini, sailing over six-foot jumps on graceful Thoroughbreds. After college she leased a small horse farm in East Hampton and taught people how to ride. Her most memorable pupil was Marilyn Monroe, who lived on the adjacent property for a while with her husband Arthur Miller. Mimi remembers that the riding lessons were Miller's idea—he wanted to ride side-by-side, holding hands with his bride— but that Marilyn was scared to death of the horses.

Mimi herself gives the impression of being rather fearless, of animals as well as of people. After ten years in the dog-eat-dog world of New York publishing, where she became editor-in-chief of children's books for Harcourt Brace and worked as a publicist for Random House, she moved out of the city and devoted herself full-time to her first love, horses. In her early twenties, Mimi trained horses and riders that went on to the Olympic equestrian games and fox hunted in Virginia alongside Jacqueline Onassis, but she prefers to spend her social life with those who are not "pink and green"—her shorthand for the Greenwich–Palm Beach crowd who are at the heart of the horsey set. Before the Bullmastiffs, she was deeply involved in the Westchester County horse world, as a licensed horse show judge and trainer. But one day she got sick of the spoiled people and pretentious attitudes of the whole scene, and she up and quit.

With this turnaround, Mimi and her husband Arthur, a New York advertising executive, and their three children, moved into a newly constructed house in the wooded back country of Westchester County. Always a dog lover and owner of a "collection" of rescued dogs, large and small, Mimi had made a checklist of what her perfect dog would be: large but not giant, protective but not crazy, with natural (uncropped) ears and tail, and short-coated. Bullmastiffs perfectly filled the bill; and instead of a horse barn, the house featured a ten-run dog kennel in a free-standing building. Mimi had fallen in love with Bullmastiffs, and the dog runs were to be part of a new venture she longed to start, Allstar Bullmastiffs.

The Allstar Kennel, like the Einsteins' house, is a spacious modern place with red-stained barnboard walls. A hand-carved wooden ALLSTAR BULLMASTIFFS sign near the door shows a handsome bas-relief dog. Inside the kennel is a row of four-by-six-foot runs, each of which has an attached four-by-twenty-foot outdoor exercise area so the dogs can go in and out at will. The runs contain indestructible metal water buckets, pads for the dogs to recline on, and toys to play with. The kennel is almost surgically tidy, although unsterile in its decor, which consists of hundreds of prize blue ribbons on the wall along with photographs showing Allstar dogs winning shows from coast to coast. Shelves and cabinets hold multitudes of medical supplies as well as breeding and grooming tools; and a washer-dryer set is used for cleaning dog bedding and towels. Mimi employs kennel help to clean the runs, shovel snow, and feed, water, and medicate the dogs kept here.

All of Mimi's dogs have names that begin with the word Allstar. Once they or any dog wins its championship, "Ch."

becomes the official beginning of the name to signify their accomplishment (i.e., "Ch. Allstar's Terry Thomas"—a practice we have eliminated in this book for the sake of readability). All show dogs have ornamental titles that function as a code to encourage breed aficionados to remember the exalted ancestry behind them. In every case, the name reveals the kennel of origin—in the case of Mimi's dogs, Allstar; and they also usually refer directly to a well-known sire or dam. Avonlea's Storybook Goodfella, for example, a hefty young male entered in the Open Dog class at Trenton, was sired by Allstar's Mugsy Malone, who is one of the top-winning Bullmastiffs in recent history. The son's name echoes his father's gangster moniker and—it is hoped—reminds the judge that he is looking at the spawn of greatness. Most breeders like their bloodlines to be instantly identifiable by name, so they give all the dogs they breed names with something in common. Mimi Einstein's Allstars were all originally named after Broadway musicals—Tailwynde's Kiss Me Kate and Allstar's Pal Joey were two of her early champions—but then she began including other celebrities and fictional luminaries as well, such as Sam, who is named after the piano player in the movie *Casablanca.* Allstar's Sugar of Abbey Road is out of Allstar's Hot Honey Harlow, but her name refers to Abbey Road Bullmastiffs of Pasadena, California, where Honey is currently a brood bitch. Mimi actually wanted to name her Allstar's Sugar Kane of Abbey Road, "Sugar Kane" referring to the character played by Marilyn Monroe in *Some Like It Hot,* but that name proved too long to fit on the American Kennel Club's registration form.

The dog population of Mimi's kennel as well as of her house varies from litter to litter, season to season. But no matter how many there are on the premises at any one time, there are always two categories: house dogs and kennel dogs. It is rare for one to become another. Sam, for example, would waste away in a kennel run. Accustomed to a life of leisure, lounging on a comfy ottoman in front of the fireplace, he is the ultimate householder. He enjoys a daily breakfast of bacon and eggs, cooked for him personally by Mimi; and at night, he climbs into bed with her whenever her husband Arthur is out of town or too tired to kick him out.

Kennel dogs lead a more spartan life. They live in runs when they are not in a motel room waiting for a dog show. Like professional soldiers, dogs accustomed to the kennel need fewer creature comforts than those who live in luxury inside the house. They are less prone to separation anxieties and the stress of being taken on the road by a handler, when they have to spend hours in a metal crate. They are also less emotionally dependent than house dogs, who learn to thrive on human companionship and can be more difficult to discipline on the hectic battlefield of the show ring.

Mimi's kennel dogs are remedial, at best, when it comes to manners. Unlike the well-socialized house dogs, they simply don't know what to do in a civilized setting other than a dog show ring, a motel, or a van. We observed this one day when Mimi stopped by our house with one of her stud dogs, All-star's Ron Howard, en route to a veterinary appointment. We invited her to bring Howie in with her.

"Are you sure you want him inside?" she asked. "He's never been in a house before."

"Sure," said we, having tousled with our share of ill-behaved puppies. Forewarned but curious, we escorted Howie through the door. Two years old and a strapping one hundred sixty pounds, he looked around the living room for a long, delicious moment, then quickly set to work. He unleashed cascades of pee on a chair leg and the couch. He knocked over a setee. He overturned the coffee table, scattering cups and snacks on the floor. Too busy even to eat what had spilled, he leapt onto another couch where he discovered how easy it is to pull the stuffing out of toss pillows, flinging several opened-up ones into the air like a juggler on the old Ed Sullivan show, sending clouds of fluffy down through the room. All this happened so fast and with such unbridled canine glee that we stood gape-mouthed and in awe, laughing in horror at how easily and quickly he had turned our living room into utter chaos. Like a hippopotamus in a tea parlor, he meant no harm. He was simply a huge, wild animal who had no idea what a home was, having lived his life in kennel runs and crates.

"He's never been in a home before," Mimi repeated, chasing after the leash that had been pulled out of her hand effortlessly. "He is a kennel dog."

Whether kennel dog or house dog, all Allstar Bullmastiffs are pampered. Even the occasional runt fated to be a mere pet or the rescued reject from an abusive home is fussed over as if it were a member of an endangered species. Like most people who seriously show dogs, Mimi Einstein dotes on her kennel's offspring because her goal is the perfection of the breed. Making money by breeding and selling puppies is simply an afterthought that might help defray some of the expenses of showing. Although the cost of a well-pedigreed dog can be high—Mimi charges between $1,000 and $3,000 for a Bullmastiff puppy with show potential—and stud fees are usually in the $1,000 range, big profits are virtually unheard-of among top breeders. It is only "puppy mills" that are lucrative, by breeding willy-nilly with little concern for the gene pool, often passing on and even amplifying hereditary weaknesses in the dogs they market via pet shops. Fortunately for Bullmastiffs, they have never gotten popular enough to encourage such harmful mass production, a fate that has, in the past, befallen Collies, Cocker Spaniels, and German Shepherds, and, more recently, Akitas and Shar-Peis. As a breed, the fate of Bullmastiffs is still in the hands of those who sincerely care about the well-being of the animals they produce.

In fact, if you want an Allstar dog, you need more than money. The waiting list to buy one is long; and if your number comes up, it isn't simply a matter of giving Mimi the cash and going home with a puppy. First, you will go to her house for an interview. You will sit on the sofa next to Sam's ottoman and discuss your plans for the dog: what you will feed it, how you will play with it, what toys you will buy it, where it will sleep, and who you will call in case of emergencies. Like a vigilant parent giving away an only daughter in marriage, Mimi listens closely to make sure your intentions are good and honorable; but more important than listening, she watches. As you sit on a chair or couch, house dogs will crowd around: flatulent old veterans, bothersome puppies, cranky bitches with baggy teats, retired studs. Some will drool on you, some will try to nonchalantly elbow you to the side so they can get the better part of the couch cushion. It's fine to nudge, tug, and shove a dog to keep your share of the couch, or even to shoo one away if its hot breath is steaming up your spectacles, but if you recoil in disgust at the dogs' forwardness or shriek at their blobs of drool, or if you appear not to enjoy their company enough, you fail the test. Mimi will not sell you a dog.

Most people who breed dogs for a hobby are concerned that the puppies they produce will be happy, but really serious dog breeders are far more particular than that. "My first priority is the home the dog goes to," Mimi says before reeling off a list of qualifications that is a totally personal combination of logic, passion, and whim. "If a man calls and he is married, I want to meet the wife. If there are kids, I want to meet them. Actually, the ideal owners don't have children: the dog will be more important to them. I am suspicious of people who say they have huge amounts of property. Too often that means that the dog will run unattended and wind up run over. I don't sell to people who have invisible electric fencing. I don't like devices. I don't like buyers who come here and say they want to breed dogs. They don't have a clue what is involved. And I will not sell to someone who works all day," she says, declaring it unfair for a dog to be left alone that long. One would think that any breeder who is so persnickety would have few people interested in the puppies they produce. But breed aficionados who set their sights on a particular kennel's get can be as determined as passionate antique collectors. The obstacles Mimi sets are never too high to dissuade those who are intent on taking home an Allstar dog.

"I told one couple I wouldn't sell them a dog until their child was civilized. They had this hideous two-year-old with them. Amazingly, they waited a year and came back to show me how well-behaved the child had become. I sold them a dog then."

Some people never even make it to the personal interview. "One man called to ask if my Bullmastiffs drooled. I told them of course they do, and he said that wouldn't be a problem because he could have 'the operation' done on them. I don't know what the hell he meant, but I hung up on him.

"Another couple drove for hours to come here, from upstate New York. They sounded fine on the phone, but in person they were the worst-looking sort of people and they handled the puppies in a rough and uncaring manner. I told them they couldn't have a dog from me; but I felt sorry for them, having driven so far, so I placed a call to a breeder I knew who had a litter for sale way out on Long Island. They drove out, another five hours in the car. Late that night, they were back, knocking on my door. The Long Island breeder also hated them on sight and refused to sell them a dog, and now the man was so mad I thought he was going to break down my door and kill me. The only thing that saved me was that his wife was in the car moaning with a terrible migraine and he finally had to drive her away."

Mimi has far more requests for dogs than she could ever fulfill, so she plays with her waiting list like Scarlett O'Hara with a dance card full of admirers, offering some hope to one, snubbing another, flirting with an interesting possibility, and dropping the annoying ones to the bottom.

Because they are some of the best Bullmastiffs being bred today, Allstar dogs are sought not only by professional breeders who want to improve their own kennel's bloodlines, but also by anyone who decides they want the ultimate gamekeeper's night dog—big and typey, awesome and unflappable. Mimi has people all over the world who want her puppies. A while ago she arranged for a son of Allstar's Play It Again Sam to go to Gary Larson, creator of "The Far Side," the cartoon feature that depended so heavily on the thoughts of wonderfully anthropomorphized animals. Although dogs were the source of so much of Larson's art, the Allstar brindle boy he and his wife Toni bought was their first canine. Mimi reports that the calls to her from his Seattle home have been unbridled in their joy, and he recently called her looking for another dog to keep their first one company.

Less jubilant was the battle royale that sprang up several years ago between Mimi and prizefighter Mike Tyson. Shortly after Tyson married Robin Givens, his "people" contacted Mimi about acquiring a dog for the couple's home in New Jersey. Apparently Tyson was an admirer of Sylvester Stallone's movie *Rocky* and had become smitten by Rocky's dog Butkus, a red male Bullmastiff who also appeared in the sequel, *Rocky 2*. Mimi knew that the Tysons would not have time to take adequate care of a dog; but after meeting the South American couple in their employ who would be responsible for the dog's care, Mimi agreed to sell them a puppy from a new litter. They would be the ones who would housebreak it, walk it, feed it, and handle all the other mundane tasks of dog ownership. The dog, named Allstar's Mel Gibson, was to be picked up from her kennel when it was eight weeks old and taken to live with the heavyweight champ. Mimi volunteered to bring the puppy to Tyson and set it up in his mansion to make sure it was happy, but the people in Tyson's camp insisted on coming to pick it up. A long white limousine pulled into her driveway, with no one in it but the driver. "I'm here for the dog," the chauffeur said, placing the plump little Bullmastiff in the cavernous depths of the otherwise empty car.

Afraid Mel Gibson would arrive in New Jersey to equally empty arms, Mimi jumped in her own car and tailed the limo to Tyson's mansion, where she was met not by the fighter, his wife, or the fighter's mother-in-law, but by the couple who would be taking care of the dog. After a lengthy instructional session with the pair, Mimi left the puppy behind and drove home.

A few months passed. Mimi received a frantic phone call from the couple, who had just been fired and ordered to vacate the house as quickly as they could pack their bags. In broken English they said they were calling on behalf of the puppy, whom they had grown to love. They feared that in their absence, no one would take care of him.

Mimi once again pointed her car toward New Jersey, driving fast and smoking hard. She pulled into the driveway of Tyson's mansion and marched in the front door of his house to confront a living room full of various cronies, bodyguards, and staff. "Where's the dog?" she said firmly.

She had the element of surprise on her side. No one expected her, and no one quite knew what to do with her.

Pushing her way through the phalanx of muscle and scowls, Mimi located the dog, which had been tied in the kitchen and left unattended. In Mimi's eyes, tying up a dog is cruel and dangerous, so she untethered him, snapped a leash to his collar, and led him out to her car. It was only on the highway heading back to her kennel that she began to contemplate exactly what she had done: broken into the home of the heavyweight champion of the world and absconded with his dog.

When she walked in her door, the puppy tagging behind, the phone was ringing. "The next few weeks the phone never stopped ringing," she remembers with a strange mix of glee and panic. "I think I got a call from everyone in the fight world, Tyson himself, Robin Givens, the mother-in-law, his lawyers, his henchman. They all threatened to do awful things to me if I didn't give them back the dog. I, in turn, gave them a list of conditions they had to meet for me to return it—the same sorts of standards I hold people to in my rescue work at the SPCA. They lost interest. Arthur and I installed a security system in our house, then tried to forget about the threats. Eventually their calls stopped. I mean, frankly, I don't give a damn if it was Mike Tyson or anyone else. If a dog of mine is not treated well, I take it back!"

CHAPTER 3

How a Dog Show Works

For every breed of dog that the American Kennel Club recognizes—approximately 150 out of a world total of some 300 different ones—there is a standard. Written and updated by each breed's national club and published by the AKC, the standard is the official gage used to evaluate members of the breed. When any group of dogs go into the ring to compete in a conformation show, whether all-breed or a single-breed "specialty" show, they are, technically speaking, not competing with one another, but with the standard, against which each of them is measured.

Breed standards are primarily physical descriptions, excruciatingly detailed, specifying such matters as proper weight and height, length of nose, breadth of head, color of coat, shape of feet, turn of forelegs, angle of hind legs, tail set, tail shape, and tail movement, as well as general demeanor and disposition. For every part of a dog, there is a whole lexicon of terms used by breeders and judges to describe it precisely. Ears, for example, can be cropped, pricked, or semipricked. They can be button ears, bat ears, rose ears, or hanging ears. A crank tail is almost always a fault (except on a Bulldog, unless it is more of a sickle tail than a crank tail). There are gay tails, ring tails, squirrel tails, rat tails, otter tails, saber tails, plume tails, docked tails (trimmed), and bobbed tails (gone). Heads can be blocky, cheeky, jowly, froggy, down-faced, dish-faced, snipey, domed, Roman, or wedgy.

Every serious breeder hopes for dogs that fit the standard in every way, but it is also possible to produce ones that seem too perfect. Around dog show rings, one often hears disparaging remarks about certain dogs being "too typey"—i.e., a disturbingly massive Saint Bernard or a gaunt Whippet—in the same way a body builder can appear too bulked up, or a beauty pageant contestant over ripe.

In every case, the standard reflects what a particular breed of dog was originally designed to do, even if few members of the breed do it anymore. For example, Newfoundlands are required to have webbed feet so they can swim with enough power to pull the tow lines of fishing boats. A Bull Terrier's egg-shaped head gives it a grip like a vice against opponents in the fighting pit. A Poodle's poufs of fur were originally designed to insulate its joints when it slogged through cold, swampy terrain going after game birds. The show clip on champion Poodles is an extreme exaggeration of the once-functional hunting dog haircut. Even the scrappy personality of pint-size Chihuahuas has a logic: Bred by Aztecs to be sacrificed, their high-spirited nature was supposed to make them unfailing guides for dead humans on their way to the Other World.

In a March 1996 *AKC Gazette* story about the historical origins of breed standards, judge Edd Bivin said it was important to know not only a breed's country of origin, but also "the characteristics of the people who developed and nurtured the breed." He offered the Welsh Terrier as an example, originally developed in "a rugged land inhabited by a tough and frugal people who have little or no tolerance for anything fancy." His conclusion was that "the breed by type was—and still should be—a solidly built, determined-looking and -acting dog. If a Welsh resembles its fancier friend the Fox Terrier, the Welsh is wrong in type."

Bill Shelton, primarily a working breed judge, explained the importance of breed history as being similar to the "original intent" often cited by judges and legislators when interpreting the Constitution: a set of principles that can be used to interpret the law. He wrote, "Breed histories convey crucial details that assist judges in evaluating dogs—details that the written standard was never intended to do. . . . Great insight into a breed's intellect and anatomical characteristics can be found in history." The standard for the Bullmastiff, which Mr. Shelton frequently judges, is a good example of how a judge needs to get behind what is written to know original intent. It states simply that a dog may be red, fawn, or brindle, and except for a very small white spot on the chest, a white marking is a fault. Arbitrary? Certainly not, not if you know that the breed was originally developed to prowl around at night, unseen by intruders. A white patch positioned on the fur in such a way that it would disclose the dog would make it a poorly coated Bullmastiff. Not because the standard says so, but because it might alert a prowler to the dog's presence, allowing the interloper to draw a bead on the dog and shoot it before the dog had a chance to attack. As for intellect, the standard demands that a Bullmastiff be fearless and alert, yet docile. These are terms that could be interpreted in many ways, but when you know that the Bullmastiff was originally bred to be a gamekeeper's companion, ever-vigilant for trespassers and yet happy to spend long hours curled up by a fireplace, you have a better sense of the disposition an ideal Bullmastiff ought to have.

Although each standard is precise, judging dogs is one of the most subjective procedures in the world of sport. Like figure skating or gymnastics or a beauty pageant, dog show judging requires a judge to decide just how perfectly a contestant fulfills an ideal, and furthermore, whether that contestant does it with panache. However, unlike a skater, a gymnast, or a Miss America contestant who faces a whole panel of experts, a dog is evaluated by a single judge, one man or woman whom the AKC has anointed as competent to evaluate the breed.

Judges are required to know the standards of the breeds they are licensed to judge like a preacher knows the Bible. In the show ring, their power is absolute. If you do not agree with a judge's choice of which dog best fits the standard, you have no recourse but to wait for the next show and hope for a judge who interprets the standard the way you like.

Successful strategy in a dog campaign depends on knowing the judges' preferences and selecting shows overseen by those who like the traits of the dogs you are showing. On any given weekend during the show season, there might be two or three important conformation shows within driving distance and perhaps more than a dozen big ones nationwide. If you have the money to travel, as well as the experience of knowing the judges and the likely competitors in each venue, you will select the show in which your dog has the best chance of winning. AKC rules require that entries and entry fees for any show be received three weeks before the actual show date. This means that competitors knowingly enter many more shows than they could ever attend, waiting until the last moment to decide which one is going to provide their best shot at a win. Handlers, of course, tend to be very cagey about which show they are taking a particular dog to. A shrewd handler with a weak dog might give the impression that he is planning to show it in Springfield, Massachusetts, thereby encouraging stronger dogs to go to Springfield in hopes of beating him. Then at the last minute, when all of his competitors are on their way to Massachusetts, he'll head south to the show in Huntington, West Virginia, and then win there.

At any all-breed dog show, the judging process is a winnowing. First, within each breed, dogs are judged by class:

there are Puppy classes, Novice classes, a Bred by Exhibitor class, an American-bred class, then Open classes, and each of these classes is divided by sex. A blue ribbon is given to the best dog and best bitch in each class (runners-up get ribbons of red, yellow, white, etc.). Once a judge has awarded the blue ribbons in each class, all the winning bitches are judged against one another, as are all the winning dogs. From this group of winners, one Winner's Dog and one Winner's Bitch are chosen. Each of them receives a purple ribbon.

It is the purple ribbon that breeders covet most, for the Winner's Dog and Winner's Bitch each earn points—from one to five, depending on how many competitors they have defeated—and it is points that make a champion. (No points come with a mere Best in Class blue ribbon.) To become a champion, a dog must earn fifteen points under at least three different judges, and its wins must include at least two "majors" (a win of at least three points). That is why big shows are so lucrative for those in serious competition. There are enough contestants for major wins.

After the selection of Winner's Dog and Winner's Bitch, these two are then joined in the ring by entries who have already earned their championships at previous shows—these dogs are known as specials—and from this lofty group, a Best of Breed dog or bitch is chosen, along with a Best of Opposite Sex. The Best of Breed winner gets a ribbon of purple and gold.

After all the Best of Breed competitions have taken place, the best dog of each breed goes into the ring against the best dogs from all the other breeds in its group. Every breed of dog recognized by the American Kennel Club belongs to one of seven groups: Toys, Hounds, Sporting dogs, Herding dogs, Terriers, Non-sporting dogs, and Working dogs. The best of each group is chosen by a judge who has been certified by the AKC as knowledgeable about the standards of *every breed in the group.* The Best of Group winner receives a blue rosette. Exhibitors like to point out that the blue rosette means that your dog has beaten not only all the other breed winners, but has also virtually beaten all the dogs each of those winners beat. Working Group judging, for example, puts up to nineteen dogs in the ring; but each of these nineteen has defeated dozens of his or her own kind that day to get there.

Finally, the climax of activities at the end of the day is the selection of a dog that is Best in Show from among the seven group winners—this, by a judge who must be thoroughly familiar with the standard of every group. Best in Show judging is strange indeed, for it pits radically different specimens against one another. A lumbering 250-pound Mastiff that won the working group might be stacked side-by-side with the ten-inch-tall Skye who topped all the terriers, as well as a five-pound Maltese from the toy group, a Greyhound, a Cocker Spaniel, a German Shepherd, and a Keeshond. How can a judge possibly compare them? The answer is that they are not supposed to be compared to one another. Each dog must be measured only against its own standard, and the one that best fits that standard is the one that wins.

At the top levels of competition, though, an ineffable quality enters into the picture, regardless of breed: showmanship. Captain Will Judy, editor of *Dog World* magazine in the 1940s, wrote that it was actually dogs' personality, not their quality, that usually determined final outcome. "Show winners are dogs of quality that also have that extra 'it'—style, good movement, and a personality that seems to be asking every instant for the blue ribbon." A dog that appears to relish the show ring will win every time over one that appears merely to be going through its paces. Inevitably, in contests between different breeds—group judging, and best in show judging— this gives the advantage to those breeds that are naturally full of vim, like the Poodle or Cocker Spaniel. That is why Poodles and Cockers win more Best in Show awards than stolid breeds like the Saint Bernard or Clumber Spaniel.

The top dog that wins Best in Show takes home a ribbon cluster that is red, white, and blue.

These are the seven groups into which the AKC divides the breeds it recognizes:

Sporting dogs are the original show dogs, first put into competition because they had skills hunters valued. Pointers and setters locate game. Retrievers fetch it. Spaniels locate, flush, and retrieve game. Some of the most popular sporting dogs are Labradors, Golden Retrievers, and Cocker Spaniels.

Hound dogs track game. Those that do it by sight are known as sight hounds and are generally thin and elegant, i.e., Borzois, Greyhounds, and Afghans. Those that trail using scent tend to be less lithe—Bloodhounds and Basset Hounds, for example—and use their voice to alert hunters, on foot or mounted on horseback, to the direction of the game.

Working dogs are a heterogeneous group, but mostly big and well-muscled creatures bred to do a job. Some are still used in K-9 corps and, of course, as guide dogs and in search-and-rescue work. The working group includes Boxers, Great Danes, Doberman Pinschers, and Bullmastiffs.

Terrier dogs originally went to ground after vermin and most still have a high-spirited disposition that breeders refer to with pride as "corky." In the last century, terriers were crossed with larger breeds to become hunters, sport-fighting dogs, and guardians. They vary considerably in size, from Airedales to Dandie Dinmonts.

Toy dogs are small, charming, and companionable. Many of them, such as the Miniature Pinscher and Papillon, are pocket-size versions of larger breeds; and some, like the Pekinese, originated as breeds preferred by royalty.

Non-Sporting dogs are a group originally established at early dog shows to distinguish its members from competitors used for hunting. Today's non-sporting group is a sundry category of breeds designed for such diverse and mostly obsolete purposes as bull-baiting (the Bulldog) and meat for human consumption (the Chow Chow).

Herding dogs are athletic animals originally bred to use the canine's natural hunting instincts to work alongside farmers and ranchers. They include German Shepherds, Border Collies, and Australian Cattle dogs (but despite the hit movie *Babe,* never pigs).

CHAPTER 4

A Blue Ribbon in the Land of Pink and Green

By early June, precocious novices are well on their way to becoming champions; lame ducks have bitten the dust. Mimi Einstein's beloved Sam is one of those on the short road to dog show obscurity. Despite her hopes of kindling fire in the belly of the brindle giant after his two year hiatus, it is not to be. The weak leg and show ring ennui have made her decision to take him out of competition a relatively easy one. "I could finish him," she says, "finish" being a breeder's term for earning a championship. "But I would have to give him steroids to keep him sound. I won't do that; it isn't healthy."

Mimi's love of Sam is a big factor in taking him out of competition. She wants what is best for his health, but in addition to compassion, there is pride. She simply cannot bear for him to lose. "I can watch Sugar or Rusty take a beating they don't deserve, but when I see Sam ignored by a judge, I want to scream. It makes me livid, because the fact is that Sam is as close to a perfect Bullmastiff as there is."

To his great delight, Sam has regained his place on the family room couch, never more to parade around the show ring at the end of an anxious handler's leash. Now, instead of spending weekend nights in some strange motel room in a dog show town, Sam will be sleeping in bed with his darling Mimi (when that man, her husband Arthur, allows it), and the two of them will happily doze off together watching baseball games on television throughout the summer.

Despite retirement, Sam's animal magnetism cannot be ignored. People are still clamoring for his puppies, for which he makes frequent trips to a semen collection and storage facility near Boston. But it takes more than beauty, charm, and excellent sperm motility to become a champion.

Allstar is now fielding two contenders: Sugar and Rusty. Sugar has what it takes. As a competitor, she is green and in need of training, but in her first few outings, she has come home with the ribbons. Like Sam, she is a house dog; and when we first meet her she is happily ensconced on the sofa in the family room of the Einstein home, lying flat on her back snoring contentedly, four legs lolling upward in the air like syncopated saplings in a stiff breeze. Mimi lights a cigarette and regards her with an unsentimental eye: "This is not my be-all and end-all of what a beautiful Bullmastiff bitch should look like, but she is winning like crazy because she can fly around the ring."

Even an unpracticed student of dog flesh can see the difference between Sugar and Sam. If he is monumental, she is elegant. She is not by any means small—she weighs about one hundred twenty pounds, has good bones and a broad head— but there is a gracefulness about the way she is put together, a quality of supple poise that seems particularly well-suited to a bitch. Her coat is solid burnished red rather than Sam's variegated stripes. And unlike Sam, who is deep into his program of rest and relaxation, Sugar has the buoyancy of youth. Nor does it hurt, in terms of charisma, that any savvy judge who looks at her sees echoes of her sire, Mr. U's Music Man, the first Bullmastiff ever to go from Best in Breed to beat all the other top dogs in the Working Group, which includes Dobes,

Rotties, and Boxers, and earn a group win at Westminster, in 1993. Mimi explains the qualities she has that appeal to a judge: "She has a beautiful front, good angulation, she moves with her head up, and hits a long, gorgeous stride." What we notice is her soul-piercing amber eyes that, like Sam's, gaze unblinking from the dark masked face. They are the eyes of a protector, not a killer.

Mimi's other contender, Rusty, is living with handler Jane Hobson in rural New Jersey, where Jane has him on a daily fitness program that includes miles of jogging and stand-stay training for judges' inspections in the ring. Rusty didn't start out as one of Mimi's show dogs. He was sold as a pup to a dog fancier in California; a year later, when the Californian was divorced and could no longer care for him, he was returned. When she uncrated him at the airport, Mimi was impressed by what she saw. His head was broad and nicely wrinkled, his body was beautifully muscled, he had a lithe, athletic stride, and he had developed a showy personality. Unlike Sam, whose even temper at home translates into lethargy in the show ring, Rusty is an active handful, which gives him fire when he parades before the judges. In short order on the show circuit, Rusty earned his championship. Mimi's plan now is to campaign him throughout the East and rack up momentum that will make him an irresistible contender at the big indoor shows in the fall and winter.

There is a third Allstar prospect in the wings: Allstar's Sonny Boy. A six-month-old child of Sam, Sonny will be hauled to a few puppy Sweepstakes classes (a sort of test-run competition where no points are earned) to try his luck and see how he likes the ring. Sonny is a house dog and looks like he could develop into a showy character, but he is now at an age when he is mostly a pest. When Mimi returns from a long Memorial Day weekend of shows, she finds him lounging on his bed happily gnawing on a brand-new, never-worn cowboy shirt with piranhalike puppy teeth. In her absence, supervised by a distracted house-sitter, he had also pooped on four separate dog beds, rolled in the poop, then fetched her Calvin Klein blazer from the closet to shred on top of one of the soiled beds. When he grew bored destroying clothes, he managed to pull a video camera off its wall hook and chew it to smithereens. "I told one of my kennel girls to take him outside," Mimi says. "At that moment, I had to put him in the kennel for his own safety. If he had stayed in the house, I would have killed him."

Sonny, whom Mimi takes to calling Son of Sam to fit his demonic behavior, needs boot camp, so Mimi calls Jane Hobson and arranges for her to come pick him up for basic training. As Jane drives away, Mimi lets out a sigh of relief. "I cannot tell you what a joy it is for me to share the house with only mature Bullmastiffs. It is so pleasant not to have to worry every time I leave a shoe somewhere, *will that goddamned puppy eat it?*"

After a short course in Jane Hobson's brand of canine tough love, Sonny returns to Mimi's house. He is better disciplined, but at a physically awkward age. Mimi is unabashed in her appraisal of his current charms. "Sonny is hideous," she declares. "Gawky, horrible—a gangly, loping thing. He is like a thirteen-year-old boy who suddenly wakes up one morning and is six-foot-four. He doesn't know what to do with his body. He trips over his own feet." Nevertheless, her plan is to let Sonny have a preview of his life in the ring at the forthcoming puppy Sweepstakes contest at the Greenwich, Connecticut, dog show, then take him home to fill out and grow up for a year before he is brought back into the public eye. With luck, in that year he won't grow coarse-looking or fall over and cripple himself.

A Blue Ribbon in the Land of Pink and Green

The morning of the Greenwich Kennel Club Show, held June 10 on the SUNY campus in Purchase, New York, Mimi arrives looking uncharacteristically flashy. Her ubiquitous sweatshirt—usually a subdued blue, green, or purple—is today an eye-scalding pink, perhaps in honor (or as a mockery) of the Greenwich club members' preference for the dreaded "pink and green" lifestyle she eschews. Indeed, there is a preponderance of chino pants and L. L. Bean moccasins on site at this show, and the volunteers who take your money at the entrance gates all seem to share the same outdoorsy, weathered look attained from standing around horse and dog show rings, and casting fly-fishing lines into the midday sun.

The stakes today are especially high for Bullmastiffs, because Greenwich is something more than just another all-breed dog show. It is also a Bullmastiff specialty show, which means that all serious breeders in the region will bring their best dogs to see how they measure up. Seventy-three Bullmastiffs are entered in the regular classes, thirty-two in the puppy Sweepstakes that precede them. This is a tremendous entry; to win in a show this size is to win big: five full points, the most it is possible to earn in any one show. Sugar is exactly five points away from finishing her championship.

As Mimi waits for Sugar's Open Bitch class, she is approached by many people. If you are a Bullmastiff person, you know who Mimi Einstein is. She is an important breeder; Allstar bloodlines have enriched many of the top kennels in the country; and she serves on the Board of Directors of the American Bullmastiff Association. Although well-known among the Bullmastiff fancy, Mimi is an enigma to many. Her voice is whisper-low, her words are few and measured. At this specialty show, she must divide her time between intently watching the action in the ring and making the prerequisite small talk with fellow breeders and Bullmastiff fanciers.

A dog show is like a class reunion, crowded with people and dogs you love and some you hate, all of whom you're curious about. There is gossip ("Look how fat that bitch got!"), scandal ("She is sleeping with the judge!"), and intrigue (who bred what to whom?). How well the dogs do is the ostensible focus of the day, but the interaction among the breeders, handlers, and hangers-on can be every bit as fascinating.

Mimi peers over the top of her dark sunglasses to identify people she wants to make contact with and others she wants to avoid. "Oh, look, it's that disgusting man," she mutters, trying to disappear behind a tree. "Oh, Jane, look, it's that nice woman we met, what's her name? . . . I met her on that island, what's it called?" Her whispered commentary is interrupted by two Bullmastiffs she spots heading in her direction. "Oh, my God, it's Martin!" Mimi gushes with true enthusiasm. Champion Allstar's Martin Riggs and his niece Jody have come to the show not to compete, but to visit Mimi. Now owned by Mimi's friend Micky Niego, Martin is seven years old and retired, neutered, and well past his prime as a show dog. But when Mimi took him on the circuit, he was dynamite, winning the Best in Show trophy at the prestigious Twin Brooks Kennel Club show. Best in Show is a supreme honor for any dog, and an extreme rarity for a relatively scarce breed like the Bullmastiff. Martin's show career was so outstanding that to this day, his picture is the image Mimi Einstein uses on her Allstar business cards. She has never really gotten over parting with him, which she had to do because he began squabbling with another, older male house dog who had first dibs on the couch. Rather than subject Martin to kennel life, Mimi let him go to Micky.

Champion Allstar's Martin Riggs is now a certified therapy dog, and Micky proudly tells Mimi, "He has a summer job— at camp, working with autistic children." Martin is deep red, with a head bigger than a basketball and an expression sweet as candy. With age, his waist has grown thick and solid muscle has given way to softer flesh; but his most arresting feature—his penetrating gaze—hasn't dimmed at all. In fact, he was originally named by Mimi's daughter Elizabeth as a tribute to the character Mel Gibson played in *Lethal Weapon;* she thought Martin's eyes shown with the same manly intensity that makes Gibson so handsome.

Martin attracts a fan club of four strolling yuppies who have come to the Greenwich show to browse at dogs. "What breed is this?" one asks with the same kind of acquisitive intent he might use to compare BMW models in a car showroom.

As Micky Niego cheerfully explains the wonders of the Bullmastiff to the two couples, the girls kneel down and cuddle his immense head. He basks in their attention. His big, spatulate tongue is hanging out one side of his mouth and his amber eyes are gleaming in their embrace.

"God, he is so dense," says one of them, who is wearing a white Lacoste shirt on which a large pool of drool is rapidly spreading. She is oblivious to the puddle because she is so seduced by the feel of the corded muscles of Martin's broad neck. Ropes of slobber are falling on her Dockers and tennis shoes as she wraps her arms around his head.

"He's such a mess," the other girl says when she notices the dripping saliva.

"Oh, that's nothing," Micky says with mischievous glee, telling them about the slobber that hits the ceiling at home when he flaps his jowls and how she has to use a mop periodically to remove it. The yuppies rise up and hurry away, heading for the tidier retrievers in ring 14.

When they are gone Mimi cannot resist bending down to plant a kiss atop Martin's card-table-broad head. Micky and

Mimi reminisce about the time Martin was being shown at Westminster at Madison Square Garden at the height of his career. He was as thick as a little rhino and rather than stay confined in his crate, he spent the whole show in the aisle. "I thought he would lose his fur so many people came by to pet him," Mimi recalls, "but he loved it. He can never get enough petting. By the end of the show, he was so tired he was weaving back and forth on his feet."

There is one human at the show to whom Mimi gives an eye as kind as that she had for Martin. His name is Vito Ancona, and he doesn't even own a Bullmastiff. A retired union official for Carey-Greyhound, Vito is a love-him-or-hate-him kind of guy. He is in his sixties and lives in Queens with his mama. He's got a pack of unfiltered Camels in his pocket and pointy black cowboy boots on his feet, and for this show in the land of Ralph Lauren style, he arrives wearing a Hawaiian shirt in screaming fuchsia with a big green flower pattern. Bullmastiffs are Vito's hobby—not owning them, not showing them, but just *them.* He is a Bullmastiff connoisseur, a lover of the breed who indulges in the same over-the-top passion indulged by opera fans who wait at the stage door for their favorite divas. He is the ultimate drugstore cowboy, and he knows more about his favorite subject than people who do it for a living.

Vito is a fixture at Bullmastiff shows. "He has been kicking tires for years," Mimi says, referring to the fact that he loves to browse, but doesn't buy. Some breeders think he is a waste of time, and as Vito approaches groups of them, they scatter to avoid a colloquy. Mimi, however, holds her ground and gives him a good smile. She knows he is a kind soul and truly loves Bullmastiffs, loves them in a way that is so profound he can't bring himself to own one.

In truth he did own a Bullmastiff once, a dog named Case,

whom he adored. Case got cancer. Although not a rich man, Vito took him to the best animal hospital in New York and had top specialists there give him chemotherapy. But Case died anyway, and since then Vito has dedicated himself to knowing everything there is to know about the breed. "I am now legendary for my eternal search," he pronounces. "Anybody I buy a puppy from is going to be famous, because I have a reputation for not buying anything."

Mimi likes Vito because he truly likes dogs. Vito likes Mimi for the same reason. "Mimi is a credit to the breed, the epitome of breeders," he says, embarrassing her among her friends. "Do you think a guy like me would ever meet a classy lady like her any other way? What I like about Mimi is that she won't sell you a dog unless she knows you will treat it right. That's especially important with this breed. If I were a breeder, though, let me tell you, I would be worse than she is. I would come to *your* house and make sure the dog was happy. Mimi is a pleasant lady, I am a hot-headed guinea."

Vito currently owns two dogs, one a mutt he rescued from his neighborhood when somebody tossed it over a fence and he found it half-dead, hanging by a chain around its neck. He found his other dog trapped in a dark basement on his way to buy a pack of smokes. He heard it whimpering somewhere below the sidewalk and investigated, finally freeing the imprisoned dog. He also tells the story of a Doberman bitch he found on the street a while back that was so small and scrawny that "It looked like a rodent and you could see her intestines through her skin." He was going to have the dog put to sleep because she appeared to be so ill. "As I was petting her, I saw the tail wag a little, and I said *you son of a gun.* I took her home and fed her chopped meat, honey, and vitamins. She grew up to be tall and fine." Vito found a nice young couple and placed the dog with them, and he looks in on it regularly.

To Vito, Bullmastiffs are something more than dogs. They are creatures of rare beauty and charm—canine gods and goddesses. Wondering if his infatuation extends to other giant breeds, we ask him if he likes Mastiffs as well. He winds his face into an expression of great scorn, leans forward, and puts two beefy hands on our shoulders. In a conspiratorial tone low enough so that Mastiff fanciers a few rings away cannot hear, he says, "If they had done the job, we wouldn't have needed Bullmastiffs."

As we talk to Vito, a good-looking Bullmastiff walks by on a leash. Vito loses his train of thought, mesmerized by the passing dog. "What is his breeding?" he asks the handler.

"Ladybug and Moonbeam" the person replies.

Vito appears startled, as if someone told him the earth was indeed flat. "Sometimes you're surprised," he says, closely studying the handsome dog walk away. "Moonbeam . . . I never would have guessed." Vito regains his composure, smoothing the front of his gaudy shirt over his belly.

"Let me tell you about the Bullmastiff," he says, inspired by the vision of beauty that just walked past. "This is a very special breed, a breed apart.

"This is a breed with dignity, this is a dog that suffers in silence.

"This is a breed that cannot be taken for a joke.

"This is a dog with a neck that starts at thirty inches.

"This is a dog that can break your spine.

"This is a dog that must be loved!

"This is a dog who is one of the greatest psychiatrists going. You look in his face and you forget everything."

Vito is on a roll. He is rocking backward on the heels of his cowboy boots, one arm flung high in the air like Pavarotti about to hit a high note. Looking desperately for a way to close his inspired treatise, he paraphrases John F. Kennedy:

"Ask not what Bullmastiffs can do for you. Ask what you can do for Bullmastiffs."

The time for small talk has ended. The judging begins, and it is almost Sugar's turn in the ring. Her class: Open Bitch. Jane Hobson brings Sugar from the van at the end of the leash. She hands the leash to Mimi, saying "Mimi, here, bond with her." Mimi kneels down and cuddles Sugar's soft face. Sugar's big pink tongue laps Mimi's tan cheeks. When the tender moment has ended, Jane takes back the leash, heading for the ring entrance. Mimi stands alone, tension rising. She is of the school of self-protective pessimism, and declares before anything happens, "You have to understand, going into a show, that it is all bullshit. These judges are people you wouldn't ask how to cross the street, much less which is the best dog in the ring."

As Mimi lights a cigarette to calm her nerves, a fellow breeder named Ed Silva wanders over. Ed is a huge man with a kindly face. His physique is solid muscles, obviously well-tended at the gym; he looks like what might happen if Disney animators touched a magic wand to a Bullmastiff and turned him into a man for the day. Like Mimi, he fears he doesn't have a chance against the formidable reputation of handler Alan Levine and his top-winning dog, Thorn. "I am so convinced that Alan Levine's dog is going to take Best of Breed that if he doesn't, you can have the keys to my van," Ed promises.

"Normally at a specialty like this, you would see dogs from all over the country," Mimi says. "But a lot of people have been scared away. Alan Levine has such a hold on the breed that when breeders see his name, they don't even bother to show up. They know they cannot win against him."

Alan Levine stands with the bitch he is taking into the Open class, toying with his thin brown cigarillo and sizing up the other dogs around him. He ambles over to Mimi and Jane

61

to say hello, refusing to be intimidated by Mimi's frosty demeanor. Mimi and Jane soften a bit, joking with him that they have contemplated breaking his legs so he can't complete. He laughs and tells Jane that all she has to do to win is "grow a mustache and get a straw hat. That's my secret."

As he walks away, Mimi's smile fades. "Let's see how the judge can screw up this class now," she says under her breath.

Unless you are within ten inches of Mimi you cannot hear the running commentary she recites as Jane enters the ring with Sugar in a field of twelve aspiring bitches. Mimi has perfected the art of talking without moving her lips; and with eyes hidden behind dark glasses, she resembles a Secret Service agent: cryptic, alert, and wary of everything.

She is rigid with tension as Jane leads Sugar into the show ring. To dissipate the anxiety, she imagines what each dog is thinking. "This one wants to kill someone—look at her hackles—but the idiot judge is smiling," Mimi says. "What is the matter with him?" As the judge runs his hand over the next one's back, the dog twitches. "This one is saying, 'Get me out of here, don't let that bastard touch me,'" Mimi says. She translates each dog's expression and reaction as the judge methodically makes his way around. In Mimi's little psychodrama, the dogs are fully aware of the judge's fallibility, and they share her fatalistic sense that the deck is stacked against them.

Judges of dog shows are as unpopular as baseball umpires. Only one dog in the ring can get the blue ribbon, which means that the owners and handlers of all the other ones are bound to feel gypped. After all, they wouldn't likely have entered the show unless they thought they had a winner. In this competitive world, there aren't a lot of "good losers"; even many of the people who regularly take home blue ribbons delight in running down the competition and scoffing at the lameness of the judging. Nearly everyone, except perhaps the winning dog's contingent, is convinced that the judge is blind, ignorant, on the take, or has a personal vendetta against them . . . and they freely express these opinions among themselves as the show goes on.

It takes a long time for the judge to get to Sugar, and because she is still relatively new to the ring, she appears a little fidgety while waiting. But when he arrives to scrutinize her, Sugar strikes a pose. She is stately. She doesn't budge when he peels back her lips to examine her teeth, and she is oblivious to all distractions. She stands with pride, apparently delighted to be showing off: the perfect eager attitude for a show ring. When the judge asks Jane to walk her on a brisk diagonal back and forth, she lunges forward, too engrossed in the business of being perfect to pay any attention to other dogs.

"Make noise!" Mimi implores the ringside allies who stand near her as Sugar begins to move. Applause and wolf whistles are meant to let the judge know that the audience think this is one hell of a fine-looking canine. And she is. Sugar moves gloriously. She sails around the ring with spring in her step, her head high, her expression a perfect Bullmastiff blend of grandeur, diligence, and vitality. Mimi's sister Allison has come to lend support. Allison is a tall slender woman who looks like she is accustomed to applauding with ladylike claps at string quartet recitals. She is not a hooter or a hollerer, and she confesses to us that Mimi was furious at her one year when she came to the Westminster dog show and was too inhibited to make lots of noise when Mimi's dog was being judged. Today she gives her best effort, clapping loudly and making little yelps as Sugar struts past.

The moment of truth is near. All the bitches have been examined by hand and by eye, and the judge asks certain handlers to once again walk the dogs around the ring for a second look. Then he lines them up in a row. Jane Hobson, Alan

Levine, and all the handlers in the ring use every trick they know to make their dogs look sharp. They move a leg, adjust a head, smooth a tail, and wave tidbits of liver or chicken in front of the dogs' noses to grab their attention. The judge points quickly to the top four bitches. Sugar is number one. He then measures her against the first-place bitches from the other classes (Novice, Bred by Exhibitor, etc.) and declares her Winner's Bitch, awarding her the coveted purple ribbon. With this honor comes five points—precisely what she needed to become a champion. Those in Sugar's cheering section scream loudly and hug Mimi, then hug Jane and Sugar when they come dancing out of the ring. Mimi is beaming with pride, almost unbelieving that Sugar, so new in her show career, won over the large field of other bitches, thirty in all. "I have to go home and add up all her show points to be sure. This happened so fast," Mimi says. "Sugar!" she says with unrestrained affection, looking down at the Bullmastiff that is gleefully wagging not just its tail, but its whole body. "You finished in record time!"

It is part of the dog breeders' lives that they must suddenly accept the mantle of greatness when they take top prize in a show that they have declared atrocious and from a judge they have deemed cockeyed. But Mimi does it with the grace that others find as well, and she happily extends her hand to all who come to wish her well.

Sugar finishing her championship is what is important, so the fact that she shows poorly in the Best of Breed class that follows is not so painful. She is pooped—hot, panting heavily, losing her focus and trotting lackadaisically across the ring. She doesn't look like a champ anymore, but rather like a clumsy puppy who wants to go home. Rusty, however, looks great, and the judge narrows down the field to two, eliminating Alan Levine and Thorn to carefully compare Rusty to Champion Briart's Solar Power (Sunny), the number-five ranked Bullmastiff in the country, shown by his owner, Barbara Heck. The Breed win goes to Sunny.

Ed Silva comes over to congratulate Mimi on Sugar taking the Winner's Bitch blue ribbon. "Where are the keys to your van that is now mine?" Mimi winks.

Ed replies, somewhat embarrassed: "I owe a lot of people vans today." He reveals that he made the same bet with every handler in the show, except of course Alan Levine.

Mimi walks to her van to fetch the big silver trophy Challenge Cup she must now relinquish. Like the America's Cup, it is passed along each year from winner to winner. Rusty took it home from Greenwich last year; and now Mimi has to turn it over to Barbara Heck and her Briart's Solar Power. Normally, the Challenge Cup would be placed on a ringside table along with all the other ribbons and trophies, but this year Mimi intends to hand it to Barbara personally. There would be a problem putting it on display, Mimi admits as she heads toward the parking lot to retrieve it. It seems that one day not long ago Sugar and a veteran Allstar bitch named Doris Day got into a territorial dispute in Mimi's house. "I grabbed the closest thing I could find to break up the fight, and it happened to be the trophy," she explains sheepishly as she buffs its silver rim on her shirt. "I beaned Sugar on the head with it. The base got dented, and now it won't stand up straight. Do you think anyone will notice?"

CHAPTER 5

When Poodles Reigned

There is no better example of the truism that people and their pets look alike—and even act alike—than a dog show. Such stereotypes are politically incorrect, but the fact is that there are an awful lot of big, beefy folks who show big, beefy dogs; conversely, there is a preponderance of tall Borzois at the ends of leashes held by elegant sorts with aquiline features. See the beautifully groomed Scottish Terriers being handled by handsome men with Ralph Lauren sweaters draped around their shoulders? Surely, it is not mere coincidence that so many people who bring buff Boxers into the show ring look like they regularly pump iron at the gym.

When you think about it, the resemblance of people and their dogs isn't all that odd. Most dog fanciers are attracted to a breed because it reflects their taste and personality. A rough-and-tumble person isn't going to be happy in the company of aristocratic-looking Afghan Hounds; a compulsive weight-watcher would probably be horrified by a house full of tubby Bulldogs; and someone who spends hours at the beauty parlor will likely enjoy the elaborate grooming rituals associated with a rope-coated Puli. That's part of what makes a dog show so much fun for spectators: the tremendous variety of humans whose looks and attitudes resemble their dogs'.

Just as pets tend to reflect the nature of their owners, breed fashions mirror our culture's dreams. Like books at the top of the best-seller list and trendy hairstyles, dog breeds become popular because they express commonly held fantasies of how people want to look and live. For example, shortly after long-haired British rockers got popular in the swinging 1960s, Old English Sheepdogs, with fur so long it covers their eyes, came into vogue, too. The proliferation of Labradors and Golden Retrievers—dogs with a sporting image associated with gracious country life—parallels the success of the L. L. Bean catalogue in the 1980s. And the extraordinary rise of muscle-bound Rottweilers to the second-most popular of all registered breeds precisely coincides with the sales growth of home-fitness machines.

What, then, is the meaning of the Poodle, the most popular dog in America for a quarter century in post-war America—a run at the top of the charts longer than any other breed? (Even today it is among the top ten.) Fanciers say the answer is simple: The Poodle is a natural performer in contests that measure beauty or skill. But there is a bigger meaning to the Poodle's reign in postwar America; the breed's meteoric rise from oblivion into the spotlight is the quintessential example of how dog styles express the soul of culture at large.

Poodles perfectly fit the mindset of the 1950s because they could be so flamboyantly customized: their fur tinted in pastel hues like a Cadillac Coupe de Ville and clipped to be as curvaceous as Jayne Mansfield. It was an era that relished voluptuous excess, and although tinting and creative clipping were and still are forbidden in the show ring, many a Poodle outside the ring became the object of such extremist grooming. Miniature poodles, once a novelty at less than fifteen inches tall, became a rage among dog fanciers and the most popular dog in the world by the mid-1960s. Toy poodles, their even smaller brethren at less than ten inches, proliferated, too. The 1950s was fascinated by such size distortion (think of 1957's

Incredible Shrinking Man and *Amazing Colossal Man*). "Teacup" Chihuahas (so-called because they were often photographed lounging in dainty Spode cups) grew to become the third-most popular among all breeds; and at the other end of the spectrum, the extra-large "royal" Poodle enjoyed a tremendous vogue (although "royal" is not a size recognized by the breed standard).

Best of all, a Poodle was modern, which nearly everybody wanted to be in the 1950s. Then as popular culture's tastes moved from futuristic to sophisticated, the Poodle morphed as well, for sophistication seemed to be its middle name. Like a foreign art film, a gourmet meal, or a Givenchy sack dress, the Poodle became an emblem of a certain kind of good life that prized savoir faire. Indeed, it was no accident that the Poodle (erroneously known as the "French Poodle") first became the single-most popular breed in the country in 1960, the same year farm-raised Ike prepared to turn over the presidency to Jack Kennedy of Harvard and Hyannis Port. Out went Midwestern Americana; in came the closest thing this country has had to a royal family. The chic Kennedys arrived at the White House with a French chef, a French hairdo (on Jackie) by Alexandre of Paris, and a cosmopolitan flair that America adored.

The Poodle's ascension in mid-century America was a dramatic change from its earlier reputation as a useless, snooty wimp. The favorite breeds of most American dog fanciers early in the century were hunting dogs or terriers; during the First World War, one popular propaganda poster showed the German Dachshund, the Russian Borzoi, the French Bulldog, and the British Bulldog all dwarfed by a dauntless American Bull Terrier who proclaimed, "I'm neutral, BUT not afraid of any of them!" The Poodle, who had long ago forsaken his original rough-and-ready skills as a gun dog to become a gentle homebody, now had no place in that rogue's gallery of pugnacious, patriotic canines. To most Americans, a scrappy terrier like "The Little Rascals'" Petey or *The Thin Man*'s Asta was the kind of pet a man could feel proud to call his own. The Poodle, with his curly coiffure and capricious way, seemed like a pampered softy. A patriotic citizen wanted a dog who carried himself like Bogart or Cagney, not like Charles Boyer.

Opinions began to change in the 1930s, when a Poodle fancier named Helene Whitehouse Walker, vexed by the Poodle's undeserved limp-wristed reputation, devised a series of tough obedience exercises patterned after those held by the English Associated Sheep, Police, Army Dog Society and sponsored the first all-breed obedience test in America—starring Poodles, of course. Then another Poodle-loving lady named Mrs. Blake Hoyt imported a white Swiss-bred Standard Poodle named Nunsoe Duc de la Terrace of Blakeen. The Duc swept nine Best in Show awards, including Westminster in 1935—the first Poodle ever to earn the top prize at America's top show. His win was so stunning that *The New Yorker* ran an "interview" with him and Duc souvenirs were sold on New York City streets. "His vitality and size completely did away with any idea of the Poodle being a sissy or decadent," Mrs. Blake Hoyt proudly declared.

The Poodle's image was beefed up, and at the same time, society's dog cravings began to change. Although the curse of effeminacy was to a great degree lifted, the Poodle nonetheless retained its aura of refinement, which was a quality that many postwar Americans craved. Several soigné celebrities owned one, including writer Ilka Chase, whose Mr. Puffle favored chocolate-flavored rubber bones and designer "Esmé of Paris," who had nine (at one time) and who wrote in 1960, "To describe their beauty and elegance seems superfluous, since they have become The Fashion in a big way." The growing rage for Poodles was not limited to the rich and famous, or even to upwardly mobile, middle-class adults. Teenage girls fancied party skirts decorated with felt appliquéd French Poodles wearing rhinestone collars; dime stores sold cheap, sporty handbags with embroidered Poodles on the side, and sales brochures for new mobile homes boasted of breakfast-nook wallpaper with a Poodle/Eiffel Tower pattern.

In a society that was learning to value cultural refinement, a Poodle attracted all the right sort of attention. In the 1952 movie *April in Paris*, Doris Day played a corn-fed chorus girl who needs to masquerade as a diplomat. To make her point, she appears with six Standard Poodles, each dramatically clipped and dyed—two pink, two aqua, one green, and one gold. That February, just before the Westminster Kennel Club show, *The New Yorker* put a Poodle on its cover, surrounded by members of the press, silver trophies, and blue ribbons. Three years earlier, cartoonist Michael Berry drew a panel that shows a pair of fashionably dressed women walking a jaunty, well-clipped Poodle on a leash along Park Avenue. They are surrounded by high-tone gentlemen in top hats and a gaggle of press photographers, but the swank gents and pressmen focus their attention exclusively on the prancing, gay dog. "You and your cute ideas!" one gal says to the other. "Nobody has looked at us all day." The Poodle—stylish, debonair, and impossible to ignore—was a breed whose time had come.

CHAPTER 6

Dog Days

Summer's dog days are fierce. Eggs fry on the sidewalk in Phoenix; Chicagoans are dropping dead from heat prostration; and on Saturday, July 29 in Rhode Island, television weathermen warn viewers to stay indoors: the combination of temperature and humidity feels like a hundred and ten degrees in the shade. On the broad athletic fields behind East Providence High School, where there are no shade trees, a Bullmastiff named Homerun's the Yankee Clipper, competing at the Providence County Kennel Club show, is about to collapse from exhaustion.

Providence is the setting for the annual American Bullmastiff Association New England specialty show, held as part of a large all-breed show. It is an important event; top breeders of the region attend, and more than ninety of the nation's best Bullmastiffs are registered to compete. By 10:30 in the morning, when fourteen dogs enter ring 9 for the Open Dog class—males who have not yet earned their championship— it is well over ninety degrees in eighty percent humidity; and although there is some shade under a tent for spectators and waiting dogs, those in the ring have no protection from the wilting atmosphere. Because these are fourteen well-matched competitors, no quick decision can be made by Polly Smith, a breeder of American Foxhounds who has been invited up from Virginia to judge Bullmastiffs.

As is customary for a judge, Mrs. Smith runs the dogs around the ring, first as a group then individually. To accurately compare the traits of one dog to another, she asks the handlers to trot them in smaller groups and occasional pairs of two. After a half hour of such scrutiny, even young handlers in good physical condition are dripping sweat. The dogs swelter, too, and those with shorter muzzles are beginning to have trouble getting the oxygen they need and their throats are clogging up with drool. Homerun's the Yankee Clipper is distressed. When he inhales, his saliva gurgles harshly and his bright pink tongue throbs with each fast breath.

"Thank you! Thank you! Thank God!" cries Patricia List when Judge Smith points to the dog she is handling, Blazin's Boris the Warrior, as number one and hands her the blue ribbon. Mrs. List, a robust professional handler from Pennsylvania, is grateful for the win, which was what Boris needed to become a champion, but she is especially overjoyed finally to be able to leave the heat of the ring. Her partner waits at the edge with an iced towel for the dog and a bottle of Powerade fruit punch for her. "I was so red and sweaty, I bet the judge thought I was going down!" she exults as she drops the blue ribbon and grabs the cold bottle for a long draught.

All the dogs are rushed to the sidelines where they are met by friends and family members with blocks of ice, spray bottles full of cold water, and chilled blankets. But the Yankee Clipper doesn't respond to the ice cubes he is offered. He wobbles on his feet, his eyes unfocus, and he appears ready to blow, which is a term used by owners of short-muzzled dogs to describe the sudden and severe heatstroke that can afflict them.

"Ice his rectum!" Pat List calls out, pulling back from her Powerade. "Cool him from the outside in."

The suffering animal is instantly surrounded by an impromptu EMT squad. One girl applies frozen washcloths to his belly and the insides of his two back legs. Someone else holds fast-melting ice cubes to his testicles and rectum. A cold towel is wrapped around his back and neck and pieces of ice are put on his swollen tongue. A well-meaning novice comes along with a bucket of water for him to drink, but a professional handler shoos him away: if the Yankee Clipper takes in any significant quantity of cold water in this condition, the shock to his system could cause sudden bloat.

Pat List suggests a trip to a nearby pharmacy for Pedialyte—a solution used on human babies to prevent dehydration and replace lost electrolytes. "In this weather, any dog should be on electrolytes," she advises.

After a few minutes of intensive care, the dog regains his senses and is walked to his air-conditioned van to recuperate.

"These guys are working dogs, "Pat List expounds when the emergency's tension has passed. "They're supposed to be able to take it." To help her own clients take it, she packs an armory that includes two chests full of ice, fans, a generator, and chillable Polar Pads for a dog to lie on. "You must condition a dog for the summer shows," she says. "Look at Boris." She points to the newly crowned champion at her feet, who is panting, but not desperately. "Boris is fit. He stays outside, where there is no air conditioning. He is not some soft house pet. He is a competitor. That is what they pay me for—to make a dog a winner."

At Mimi Einstein's red van, which is parked less than a hundred yards away from the Bullmastiff ring, Mimi is discussing strategy with handler Jane Hobson—not ring strategy, but strategy to make sure Rusty survives the intense heat. There are six classes of bitches to judge before the Best of Breed competition in which he is entered. The wait could be well over an hour. In the back of the van, where it is dark and cool as a deep stone cave, Rusty is comfortably ensconced in his wire crate like a happy bear with gleaming eyes and toothy smile. The motor is running and an opaque silver tarpaulin is tethered over the top and along the side windows to deflect the sun. The air conditioning is set to high, and he is, for the moment, comfortable. The question is whether or not to leave the doors partially open while Jane and Mimi go to the ring and watch the judge go through the bitches. If they keep the vehicle closed, Rusty might be too cold when they take him out: The shock of emerging into the heat could knock him for a loop. In addition, there is the fear that the air conditioning could malfunction or the engine fail; in this weather, a trapped dog would die almost instantly. When they head toward the ring, they leave the side and rear doors ajar and the air conditioning at full blast; even so, Jane or Mimi walks back to check on Rusty every few minutes.

Rusty is relaxed in the back of the van; Mimi, on the other hand, is haggard and looks like a foot soldier who has spent too long in a steamy trench. "You see these clothes," she says, pointing to her wrinkled jeans and a sweat-stained blue cotton shirt rolled up at the sleeves. "These are what I wore yesterday and what I slept in last night." She spent the night in the van with Rusty, parked outside a friend's place nearby. "There wasn't really room for both of us in the house," she explains, "and I couldn't leave Rusty alone. So I bought a fan and a long extension cord and opened all the windows, but it was still hideously hot. Then the sky opened up and it poured. I watched the cord get drenched and thought we might be electrocuted. Everything inside was getting soaked, but I couldn't close any windows or we would have suffocated. When the rain stopped, mosquitoes attacked in swarms. And in the morning there wasn't enough water in the house for me to shower. All I could do was wash my face. If there is any glamour in this dog show world, it is somewhere else today."

As competition for Winner's Bitch begins, Jane goes back

to the van, where she sprays and combs her hair and smoothes down her purple print dress. She fills her bait bag with chunks of cooked calf's liver, pig's liver, and chicken gizzards. Mimi joins her at the van and helps prepare a ringside refreshment kit for Rusty: a bucket full of ice, chilled towels, the cold blanket for his back, and a spray bottle. It is close to a hundred degrees outside, but when Rusty hops out of his cage onto the parched grass of the athletic field, he looks cucumber-cool, bright-eyed, and confident, like an impeccable man whose wardrobe seems just-pressed no matter what the weather. Jane whisks a Baby Wipe over his back as she and Mimi discuss tactics: Do they want to enter the ring in the middle of the pack, so that when all the dogs trot around, Rusty runs up on the rear of the one in front of him, demonstrating his vigor? Or do they want to be the first in the ring, setting the pace? "You've been going good in front," Mimi suggests.

"That's where I'll be then," Jane says, leading Rusty to the shade of the tent adjacent to the ring entrance. It is crowded there with dogs resting in crates, spectators who cannot abide the sun, and various other breeds on leashes whose owners have come from their rings to watch the contest for best Bullmastiff. A Doberman bitch admires Rusty. She sniffs his butt and he turns around with a happy glint in his eye. "Nix!" Jane cries out to the brazen Dobe, but she ignores the command. "Excuse me, hello, excuse me, please!" Jane hollers urgently at the Doberman's owner. "Pull that dog away!" She doesn't want Rusty thinking about some shapely Dobe bitch instead of the job he has to do in the ring. Jane stuffs her cheeks with liver and clips the spray bottle of water on her belt, next to her slop rag and bait bag. The moment Best of Breed entries are called for, she dashes into the ring with Rusty to be at the head of the line. No Olympic sprinter could have beaten her to the number-one position.

Six dogs and five bitches are in contention. First judge Polly Smith has all the dogs line up and run around. Then she watches all the bitches together. Then she has Rusty and another dog run around together; then another dog assortment; then a bitch assortment.

"I don't understand what she is doing," Mimi says.

"She is earning her money," another breeder responds. "She knows she's got to work for a specialty."

"He is fading fast!" Pat List calls out to her partner at ringside as Boris pants in short, quick bursts. Exhausted from his long battle in the Open Dog class, he hasn't much reserve for Best of Breed. "Hand me the Big Squirt," Pat cries. "Pump it up!" The Big Squirt is part of her arsenal: a heavy-duty plant sprayer that she uses to spritz cool vapor in Boris's mouth, on his head, and on his genitalia while the judge is inspecting other dogs.

The judge appears to have made up her mind. She sends Rusty running around the ring with Champion Laurelwoods She's A Lady just behind. Halfway around, she points to Rusty as the winner. Jane takes all the pieces of liver out of her cheeks and throws them in the air like confetti as she gleefully runs Rusty toward the ring exit. He is hardly panting.

"He is very fit," Mimi says, so delighted by the victory that she scarcely knows what to say. Other breeders and handlers come to hug and kiss her and offer congratulations, and she thanks them all. Uncharacteristically, Mimi is choked with emotion. Aside from the points and the prestige and the big silver trophy she gets, there is something deeply gratifying about a Best of Breed win at a large specialty show, among her peers, among her friends and her rivals.

"The judge wants champagne," Jane says. But there is no champagne. Instead, Bullmastiff breeder Ken Vargas has brought a large cooler full of bottled beer, much of which he made himself. The home brew is currently unlabeled, but Ken can tell by the bottle cap which batch is which, and he selects an especially good, cold one for the judge. When complimented on one heavily hopped bottle, he boasts that he recently took Best in Show at a beerfest with his chocolate stout.

As the beer is broken out to celebrate Rusty's win, a buffet provided by the New England Bullmastiff Association is set up with cold cuts for sandwiches, pasta salads, cupcakes, and a large sheet cake that says HAPPY BIRTHDAY MILDRED and has a picture of a Bullmastiff on top, surrounded by piped-on icing. Everyone sings "Happy Birthday" to the woman named Mildred, an NEBA member, then a raffle begins for prizes ranging from dog vitamins to kennel-management computer software to a small wooden end table with a portrait of a Bullmastiff painted on it. Much beer is drunk, dogs happily munch ice cubes, and the competitive spirit that prevailed all morning quickly transforms into the joyful camaraderie of people who all share a deep affection for one wonderful breed of dog. The air isn't any cooler, but with the heat of the show behind them, Bullmastiffs and their fanciers breathe easier and get comfortable.

Judge Smith sits on a folding chair in a circle with Mimi Einstein and a group of other breeders explaining her preferences in Bullmastiffs and reminiscing about earlier times in dog breeding, when each kennel was known for certain particular traits. "If you needed better head size, there was a kennel you could breed to, and get it," she says. "Or if you needed more fluid movement, certain bloodlines could be counted on for that." Now, however, kennels are smaller; and breed traits are more homogenized, she believes. When she is asked about her own Foxhound kennel, she says *American* Foxhounds, please," to distinguish what she breeds from the English Foxhound, which is somewhat heavier.

"I used to hunt behind them," Mimi says, recalling her equestrian days in Virginia. She compares notes with Polly Smith on the differences between dogs bred for field work and those bred for shows.

The easy-going revelry is rudely interrupted by a pack of tall Russian hounds and their people. Borzois are scheduled to enter ring 9 at 12:45 P.M. The large contingent of Bullmastiff people are still having their raffle, eating cold cuts, and socializing . . . and occupying nearly all the shady area under the tent adjacent to the ring. The woman scheduled to judge the Borzoi Sweepstakes orders them out to make room for the elegant coursing dogs that were originally bred to withstand Russian winters, but are light-framed enough to also thrive in the heat.

The exit order is met with considerable annoyance. "It is inconsiderate to ask all these Bullmastiffs to rot in the sun so your long-nosed Borzois can enjoy the shade," someone says.

"Never mind that. I must ask you to move," the judge says, stepping over a snoring Bullmastiff whose four legs are splayed out on a Polar Pad to keep his stomach cool.

"What kind of judge is *she?*" a Bullmastiff breeder scoffs in a stage whisper. "She drew less than twenty entries!"

"They don't even have enough for a major!" another Bullmastiff person jeers as he and several others grudgingly move into the sun to make room for the Borzois.

"Bullmastiff people have no manners!" the judge announces loudly before calling six-to-nine-month-old puppy dogs into the show ring so the Borzoi battles can begin.

CHAPTER 7

Bizarre Breeds

On the grass of Haddam Meadows State Park, by the banks of the stately Connecticut River, there is a dog show each September. The setting is quaint Americana: five small rings, a half-dozen striped canvas tents flapping in the breeze, clear air, and a china blue sky. Norman Rockwell might have painted it; but the dogs who have come, and their owners, are straight from Lewis Carroll. This show, sponsored by the American Rare Breed Association, is a trip through the canine looking glass. ARBA is a club for owners and fanciers of types of dogs that the American Kennel Club does not recognize.

If you are a casual dog fancier, you won't recognize them, either. You know a Rottweiler from a Cairn Terrier, and you might be able to tell an English Setter from an Irish one, but can you separate a Plott Hound from Foo Dog? Have you ever even heard of an Akbash, a Rastreador Brasileiro, a Glen of Imaal Terrier, or a Nova Scotia Duck Tolling Retriever? And who among us can honestly say that we can tell a really good Norrbottenspets from a mediocre one?

For those who own such dogs, a rare breed show is an opportunity to spend time with people who won't necessarily start a conversation by looking at the creature at the end of their leash and asking, "What the hell is that?"

Like the dogs they prize, many rare breed owners are different, a fact that is apparent from a mere glance around the show. There appear to be far more people of color than at an AKC show; perhaps it is because the conspicuous minority status of their preferred breeds jibes with their own situation in society at large. There are also plenty of people who speak with European or Hispanic accents and who treasure dogs from their ancestral homeland that are almost nonexistent in the USA. Among the peripheral types who attend the show are shaggy-bearded mountain men and steel-eyed survivalists in military garb, accompanied by canines who reflect their own self-image as dangerous outsiders. In fact, many of the rare breeds, such as the Louisiana Catahoula Leopard dog or the Shiloh Shepherd, have a long history in this country as hunters and companions of backwoodsmen who choose to live self-sufficient lives not sanctioned or regulated by any big national organization, including the AKC.

Earnest rare breed enthusiasts relish explaining the logic that keeps them outside the AKC. Whereas the AKC functions as a registry—publishing (and copyrighting) each recognized breed standard, but in no way enforcing it—many of the rare breed clubs *do* rigorously enforce their standards, forbidding anyone to register a dog with their club unless that dog is endorsed by recognized judges and, in some instances, vet-checked for congenital canine disorders. The AKC basically permits the registration of any dog with registered parents (unless an individual breeder determines that a dog is not suitable for breeding, in which case it may be sold with a "limited registration" certificate, meaning that its offspring cannot be registered). "AKC registration is no more meaningful than the *Good Housekeeping* seal of approval," one rare breed fancier scoffed. "Any puppy mill can churn out AKC-registered dogs, and uninformed people who buy them really think they are getting something special. In our club, you cannot register a puppy until three certified club members approve it, and it's been x-rayed, and it has passed a battery of veterinary tests. In this way, we keep control of the breeding, which is how it ought to be. After all, we are the ones who care for the breed, certainly more than a bunch of power-hungry bureaucrats back East."

It isn't only libertarian principles, race, ethnicity, and demographics that make rare breed people different. The plain fact is that oddball dogs tend to attract oddballs. Not that AKC-sanctioned shows don't have their share of strange-looking people, but for the ARBA show, Haddam Meadow Park is a carnival of characters on the fringe, people who savor their standing outside ordinary life and choose a dog to broadcast it. There are bikers with spiked-collar Bulldogs, dominatrices with German Pinschers, nerds with Hairless Terriers, shaved-headed hillbillies with long-haired Whippets, and Chanel-suited fashion plates with Braques d'Auvergnes.

While most of these dogs are like nothing you've ever seen, a few of the rare breeds are recognizable even to untrained eyes. Thanks to the Tom Hanks comedy *Turner and Hooch,* movie fans know the large and exuberantly slobbery Dogue de Bordeaux, one of which played Hanks's canine sidekick. There are many Bulldog types in attendance, of several breeds, some of whom we have seen identified as "criminally inclined Pit Bulls" by lurid tabloid journalists. In person, these seem like perfectly pleasant characters, but the fact is that their fighting heritage does encourage some bad people to train some specimens for the blood sport of dog-to-dog pit fighting.

Many of the animals at a rare breed show look vaguely familiar. If you didn't know they were pedigreed, you might guess they were accidental mutts—a patchwork of breed characteristics as crazy as the Flub-a-Dub from "Howdy Doody." At this show, you see Rottweiler bodies sprouting

Bulldog heads, pooches that look like leopards and lions, dogs bred to be so lean that each and every rib is clearly discernible beneath their taut skin, mop-top Whippets, and hairless bug-eyed critters with webbed feet and transparent ears that look more like belfry bats than canine companions.

A great many of the breeds of the ARBA show fall into a class that might be called "living gargoyles." Huge, drooling descendants of the Mastiff, most of them first developed centuries ago to fight or to guard, they are now frequently used by those who own them as personal protection against trespassers and muggers. Unlike a handgun, a dog is almost always legal to have by one's side; any criminal who finds himself face-to-face with one of these creatures is going to feel like he is looking at the wrong end of a .45.

Baritone's Just a Gigolo—Gigolo for short—is a four-year-old Neapolitan Mastiff who weighs about a hundred and fifty pounds and has a huge, forbidding head with a jawspan like a great white shark. He is short-coated, charcoal black with slitty eyes that are rimmed blood red, and he has folds of skin hanging from his neck nearly to the ground. Both ears have been surgically removed, leaving only pointy stumps. His growl is a slavering, feral rumble, and his lips drip thick globs of drool which his owner and handler, Carol Paulson, describes as being the consistency of egg whites.

Mrs. Paulson, who says she lives "spitting distance" from Canada in rural upstate New York, recalls Gigolo's arrival when he was shipped to her at age two—her first Neapolitan Mastiff. "When he came off the plane in Syracuse, his crate was held together by ropes. He had torn it apart in transit. He would not get in the car until we set up a ramp. When we got him home and in his cage, he decided he never wanted to come out. Finally, I called his breeder. I had her on the cordless phone which I held up to his cage so she could yell at him.

When that didn't work, she told me to grab his collar and yank him out. I said, 'No, thank you. I like my arms just where they are.'"

Owning a Neapolitan Mastiff proved an educational experience for Mrs. Paulson. "No one told us they were dog-to-dog aggressive," she says. "A friend of mine tried to break up a fight between two of them and she wound up in the hospital. They bit her down to the bone."

A rocky start did not sour Mrs. Paulson on the descendants of the ancient Roman Mollossus one bit, and she now breeds them at her La Tutela Kennels. She gazes down at Gigolo and strokes the gristly remnants of his ear flaps. He looks up at her devotedly with pale yellow eyes. "Gigolo has never been allowed to get dog-to-dog aggressive, which is why we can show him," she says. "Once they get a taste of another dog's blood, there is no stopping them." She does admit that he can be picky about who comes near him. "He didn't like the judge yesterday at all," she says on the second day of the show. "He backed up and sat down. Today, the judge was a woman, and he liked her fine. He's more a lady's dog, anyway. At home when we watch TV, he sits next to me and our bitch sits by my husband. To prevent violence, we allow only two dogs in the house at any one time."

Another Italian-ancestored variation on the Mastiff theme is the Cane Corso, once bred for fighting. Looking at his massive jaws, severely cropped ears, and sinister narrow eyes, you would not think he was much of a cuddlebunny, but the man holding him on a leash defends him as "good with children and an easy keeper. He will protect you if the need arises, but the good thing about him is that when the threat stops, so does he. He will not go completely berserk like some of these other breeds." The man explains the extreme ear job as "a tribute to fighting days," because long ears only gave an opponent something to grab; furthermore, if an ear was torn, its blood could flow into the fighter's eyes, hampering his vision. Like many people who favor scary-looking dogs, the gentleman showing the Cane Corso is himself a formidable being. He has a military haircut, a tight T-shirt with sleeves rolled up to reveal bulging muscles and insolent tattoos, and a taut posture that appears to be in a perpetual karate stance. He explains that he has learned much of what he knows about canine species by reading *Pit Bulls & Tenacious Guard Dogs* written by Dr. Carl Semencic.

Although its entry of 147 dogs is small by the standards of major AKC events, the Nutmeg Classic Rare Breed show draws fanciers from far away. Dr. Antonio J. Gallardo comes from Rio Piedras in Puerto Rico, where he has an Ob-Gyn practice and also operates Gran Tenerife Kennels, a top producer of the Perro de Presa Canario. The Presa, as it is known to its fans, goes by many names: The Canary Island dog, the Gripping dog, the Rough dog, or Verdino. Originally brought to the Canary Islands in the sixteenth century by Spanish conquistadors, it was bred for combat and today on the islands some of its progeny still run wild and are greatly feared for their habit of coming down from their dens on the volcanic slopes to eat people's sheep, cattle, and children.

Dr. Gallardo, himself an immense figure of a man, comes prepared to graciously field the kind of dilettante inquiries all rare breed people get. To interested parties, he distributes a multipage photocopied document headlined *Racial Profile of The Canary Island Gripping Dog,* which describes the Presa in semiscientific terms: "Large head, squarish appearance and wide cranium. Lower lips covered by upper lips. Black mucous membranes. Strong teeth, widely spread and strongly anchored. Cylindrical neck, strongly muscled and covered by thick skin, loose and elastic. Double but not excessive chin." Under a headline *Disposition and Aptitude,* the dog is said to be "severe in looks, possessing a deep and profound bark, loving with its owners but distrustful of strangers, and an able fighter."

"These are working dogs," Dr. Gallardo explains to a group of admirers who have gathered around him and his dog Greco, the top-winning Presa in the world. Greco is a shocking sight, with an appearance more like a panther than a dog: dark and sleek, utterly focused and without a speck of frolic in his fiery eyes. "They used to help the butcher," the doctor explains, pantomiming their task by running his own large thumb across his throat like a killer with a knife. "They used to bring down bulls."

Dr. Gallardo is well aware that the Presa is still used for the blood sport of dog fighting. "I am the only breeder and owner in Puerto Rico," he says. "There are some on the West Coast that are bred for the fighting pit. I am against that."

Dr. Gallardo is taking deposits on puppies, and has come equipped with scrapbooks filled with pictures of his show dogs and their litters. The pick of the next several litters has been spoken for (at $1,800 each), but there are still some show-quality dogs available for $1,500 each, and pet-quality ones for $1,000.

Of the seven Presa Canarios entered in the ARBA show, Greco is obviously top dog. He is led into the ring by an impeccably tonsured young man who wears a stylish sports jacket and slacks. Like his handler, Greco pays no attention to other dogs in the ring, maintaining a haughty expression that says he could whip any one of them with one paw tied behind his back. This is an animal you do not want to meet in a dark alley. You don't even want him in your house, a fact Dr. Gallardo is the first to admit. "They are not good indoor dogs," he explains. "They like to chew things—furniture and wood. I left one outside and it chewed the bumpers off my Toyota."

A man from Iowa has come to show his Azawakh, which is one of the skinniest breeds of dog on earth. "The standard says you must see the last three ribs," he says, explaining that the astonishing creature he cuddles in his arms was originally developed in the Sahara desert for hunting gazelles. "Everyone always asks me if my dog is too thin," he says wearily. It is easy to understand people's concern. An Azawakh is a study in bones, like an anorectic Whippet on chopstick legs with a wasp waist tucked up high behind a spare ribcage. He is a sight you'd expect to see on the side of a donation can for the anti-cruelty society. But his owner assures passers-by, for the millionth time, that this is exactly what the breed is supposed to look like.

Every kind of dog, rare or not, has a logic to its shape and size. Ears are cropped so they won't bleed in a fight. Loose jowls and dewlaps protect the muscles of the neck. Long muzzles give better wind. The Azawakh man explains that his dog's legs are long so that heat quickly radiates away from the body in the desert. High speed is simply a side effect of the ability to cool quickly. "They can run thirty miles an hour," he boasts. "Not quite as fast as a Greyhound, but in the real world, they are much better because a Greyhound isn't agile enough. When a rabbit does a ninety-degree turn, your Azawakh will follow him precisely. A Greyhound is too heavy, so he'll continue straight ahead like a runaway bus."

What does an average American do with a dog that runs thirty miles an hour and is genetically programmed to chase gazelles across the Sahara desert? The Azawakh man does allow that his little fellow needs regular exercise, but as you will hear from owners of nearly every rare breed—except Dr. Gallardo, with his bumperless Toyota—he is also perfectly suited for the home. "I let him run twice a day," the man says. "I usually have a hard time getting him up and out the door. This dog is the world's fastest couch potato."

Bizarre Breeds

Not all rare breeds were created to hunt or fight or work. Some were food. At least that is the heritage of the Xoloitcuintli. Susan Corrone of Bethany, Connecticut, hoists little Whipporwill's Star Catcher into our arms and explains the Xolo's history. "They were bred by the Aztecs to be eaten," she says with a laugh. "But if you didn't eat it, your Xolo was buried with you so he could show you the way to heaven. Sort of like a box lunch you'd pack before a long trip." Star Catcher is very strange to behold. Being a miniature Xolo, she weighs less than a house cat. She is completely hairless, with skin the color of a decomposing corpse. She feels faintly moist and quivery; and to hold her is like holding some odd body part of a person with a fever. Fragile and vulnerable with transparent ears and bony webbed feet, she has a few stray hairs on her tail like a rat and a tiny wrinkled muzzle. Perhaps her expression of perpetual worry is the legacy of being bred to be somebody's dinner.

Like every rare breed of dog, the Xolo is its fanciers' perfect cup of tea. "Once you have one Xoloitcuintli, you have to have more," Susan Corrone declares, revealing she has nine of them at home. She gazes lovingly at the pinched smidgen of a face on her bitch, so overwhelmed with affection that she cannot help but burst out, "Isn't she beautiful?" The question is rhetorical.

CHAPTER 8

Rusty Goes to Texas
(The Dallas Specialty)

The third weekend in September, there are more beautiful Bullmastiffs in Dallas, Texas, than in any other place on earth. Over two hundred of them, half already champions, come from homes and kennels all over America to the Harvey House motel in the Dallas suburb of Plano. By Thursday night, the halls are congested with braces of them shuffling room to room; a litter of roly-poly puppies frolics in the grass around the swimming pool; heavy panting emanates from behind closed doors and booming snores rattle pictures on the walls; every tree and hydrant on the grounds outside gets marked a hundred times by swaggering males.

The annual American Bullmastiff Association's National Specialty is the premier event in the Bullmastiff world. Over the course of a three-day weekend, there are club meetings and judges' seminars; deals are struck and breedings planned by the world's top handlers and owners; and awards are given to people whose studs and brood bitches have produced the most champions. The climax comes Saturday afternoon in the motel ballroom, where the finest Bullmastiffs in the nation enter the ring so the Best of Breed can be chosen.

Some people come dogless. Bill and Fern Dittmar of New Jersey have a bitch at home named Allstar's Bette Midler they want to breed; they are hoping to find a handsome male who can service her. Grant Slater has flown in from Kent, England, with photo albums of his magnificent stud, Dajean Red Dragon, from whom he can provide chilled or frozen semen for approved American bitches. Pat O'Brien of the venerable Bullmast Kennels of California (since 1943) has no dog she wants to show just now, but she wouldn't think of missing a national specialty.

Art and Barbara Heck load three dogs in their van for the drive from upstate New York, a trip they plan to make in three days . . . until Barbara discovers her purse stolen along the way and they lose a day trying to track it down. "I don't care about the money, and the credit cards are only an inconvenience," she says. "But I had a coin with a dog on one side and a cat on the other. My father, who was not an animal person, gave it to me. It kills me to know someone will throw it away because it has no value. It is irreplaceable." Barbara's sorrow is eased by a present from her friends Susan and Bill Jackson of Bull Run Kennels when she arrives in Plano: an oil painting the Jacksons commissioned of Barbara's two hefty littermate studs, Sunny and Opie. For the rest of the weekend, the dual portrait is proudly displayed on the bureau in the Hecks' twin-bedded motel room—snug quarters occupied by the Hecks themselves, Sunny, Opie, and the young bitch they have brought. To see it, visitors traverse a maze of the three dogs' bodies stretched out snoozing on the floor, plus their crates, quilts, and stuffed play toys.

Rusty is scheduled to leave La Guardia Airport in New York at 9 A.M. on Thursday. He has flown before, and he is relaxed about the whole affair, sitting cheerfully on the cool tile floor of the terminal next to his immense travel crate as Mimi Einstein and Jane Hobson pace nervously around him. They are waiting for a porter to wheel up a cart large enough to hold the crate. The cart will be used to transport him to a truck that can take him to the tarmac where he will get loaded on the plane with the baggage.

Rusty's giant head, radiant eyes, and bulging muscles are arresting in any context; in a crowded airport at rush hour, he stops traffic. Executives drop their jaws and put down their briefcases twenty yards away to stare at him from a safe distance. Burly cops and construction men in overalls step close to admire him. "He's a really big fella!" a really big man exclaims with great pride in another well-muscled creature. Over and over again, people ask, "How much does he eat?" and "What does he weigh?" (Bullmastiffs prompt these questions so often that one year at Madison Square Garden during the Westminster Kennel Club show, Mimi hung a sign around her dog Terry Thomas's neck saying, MY NAME IS TERRY THOMAS. I EAT SIX CUPS OF FOOD A DAY. I WEIGH 150 POUNDS.) The most amazing thing about Rusty's presence is the way he provides a litmus test of people's character. Guileless four-year-old boys and girls come over unafraid to poke his sturdy sides or tickle his ears, laughing with glee when his tail begins to pound a steady beat on the tile floor. Mean-looking types—troublemakers you want to avoid in airports and other public places—steer a wide berth around him, repelled by the force field of protection he radiates.

At the gate, Mimi Einstein does not board the plane when her row is called. Needing to be sure Rusty has been loaded safely, she confers with the gate agent who makes a call to check. A man appears from the jetway. He is wearing khaki shorts and a sailor's cap with lots of spinach on the brim, like an admiral, and he introduces himself as Marty. "I am in charge of loading the plane," Marty reassures her. "Your dog is fine. I plan to load him last because the air in the baggage compartment doesn't circulate until the plane leaves the gate." With visions of Rusty gasping for air, Mimi reluctantly boards; and from her seat, she watches his crate driven up to the baggage door below. Handlers chuckle with amazement at the big face inside the snug crate as three of them heft it onto the conveyor belt. A moment later, the gate agent comes down the plane aisle, asking "Are you the dog people? He's been loaded. We can now take off."

Four hours later in Dallas, Rusty hops off the platform from his opened crate to the pavement below. "Oh, my God, he is lame!" Jane screams as he walks in wobbly circles, favoring his right front leg. She and Mimi try to reassure themselves that it is only stiffness from the flight, but they both know Rusty has had trouble with his right front shoulder before. He usually walks his way out of it with ease. They give him Ascriptin, figuring he has two full days before the Best of Breed judging Saturday afternoon. Spotting a veterinarian's office just yards away from the Harvey House when they arrive, they wonder aloud if the vet keeps weekend hours.

As they settle in for the long dog show weekend, Bullmastiff people try to figure out the sprawling suburban maze that is Plano, Texas. "This is like being in *2001*," a breeder declares that evening over a round of margaritas in the lobby of the Harvey House. "There are restaurants across the highway where people sit on terraces and watch the traffic while they eat." Built abruptly in the flatlands north of Dallas and stretched out along the multiple-lane Central Expressway, this part of Plano is like the outskirts of many quickly grown sunbelt cities: so relentlessly franchised that when you drive anywhere you feel like you are trapped in a repeating loop as you pass yet another El Chico, IHOP, McDonald's, Payless, and Sports Mart. But except for a small contingent of independent sorts who forsake a dog club business meeting to whoop it up at the Mesquite Rodeo Friday night (trading "bullshit for bull-riding," a rebellious one declares), most conventioneers never leave the motel. It is too compelling to bask in the company of so many dogs and dog people who share your passion, in an environment where for three days the Bullmastiff is celebrated as a supreme being.

The American Bullmastiff Association hasn't commandeered quite all of the Harvey House. Clusters of vacationing families and business people are sometimes spotted in the halls and lobby gaping at the dozens of big drooly dogs tramping about, most of the interlopers sharing a bemused expression that is equal parts curiosity and alarm. In a small chamber next to the Dogwood Room, in which a plastic tarp is stretched across the rug for crates and show paraphernalia, a meeting space is prepared with orderly rows of chairs and a podium for the Society of Democratic Iranians who are planning to hear a lecture from a Persian expatriate. On the other side of the Dogwood Room, which is sometimes so crowded that hordes of dogs sprawl outside in the hall, geological discussions are scheduled by the MEOR (Microbial Enhanced Oil Recovery) Group. And just down the hall, past Trinity II and Trinity III—the two dining rooms that have been combined into one huge ballroom for the dog show—there is a weekend-long inspirational seminar scheduled by a company that sells cosmetics via home parties. Those who attend the sales meeting wear nylon jackets with this inscription on the back: SHARE THE DREAM, BE DEBT FREE, ASK ME HOW. In the hotel lobby, when a Bullmastiff person makes the mistake of doing what the jacket says and asks one of the bright-eyed cosmetics drummers what the jacket means, the person begins, "Let me tell you about the most dynamic multilevel marketing company in the world today . . ." An unstoppable rote spiel continues through the motel halls as the dog person tries to get away, heading for the show ring with the cosmetics man hot on his heels. When they round the corner into the area where the Bullmastiffs are being shown, the chase halts suddenly; the salesman's pep talk winds down like a phonograph that has just lost power. "Oh, my God," he shrieks, staring at a horde of big dogs assembled in the hall, tongues and tails wagging. "We are meeting with monsters!"

The first event Friday, beginning at 7:30 in the morning, is the Futurity, at which the young get of prize animals is judged and money won by those who have placed prenatal bets on their favorite producers. Its judge is Carol Beans of Tauralan Bullmastiffs in Santa Ana, California. Carol has been a Bullmastiff fancier for twenty-six years and is the publisher of *The Bullseye,* a magazine devoted to the breed and that always includes a "Right Now" recipe for people who come home late after a dog show and don't have time to cook. One such suggestion for the busy dog owner, published in April 1995, is for Twin Ham Roll-ups:

> *1/2 cup whipping cream*
> *2 tablespoons mayonnaise or salad dressing*
> *1 tablespoon prepared horseradish*
> *1 8 1/4 ounce can crushed pineapple, drained*
> *8 slices boiled ham*
> *4 ounces liverwurst*
> *1/3 cup chopped sweet pickle*

Whip cream. Fold in mayonnaise and horseradish. Fold 2/3 of this mixture into the pineapple. Spread the pineapple mixture on four of the ham slices. Roll them up. Spread the remaining ham slices with liverwurst, then with the reserved mayonnaise/horseradish mixture. Arrange the chopped pickle down the center. Serve one pineapple-filled and one pickle-filled ham roll to each person. Serves 4.

In the room where the Futurity takes place, dog people are scouting hazards. "This is an accident waiting to happen,"

Mimi Einstein at home with Allstar's Play It Again Sam (at right) and a pesky six-month-old pup named Barry.

Therapy dog Allstar's Doris Day with a nursing-home friend whose final request was for Doris to be by her side. (From the collection of Mimi Einstein.)

English Springer Spaniels stacked for the judge. Dog shows were originally developed to evaluate sporting dogs like these.

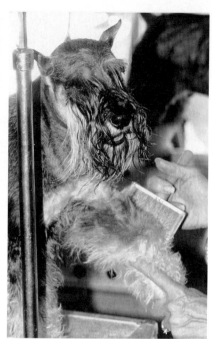

Bathing, clipping, combing, and fluffing: show dogs are readied for their turn in the ring.

After an Old English Sheepdog has been de-matted, scissored, bathed, and blown dry, a pin brush is used to attain maximum fluff.

To keep its topknot neatly parted before showtime, this well-groomed Afghan wears a snood.

The breathtaking show clip on Poodles actually descends from a practical haircut: the puffs of fur were meant to insulate joints when slogging through water after game birds.

Allstar's Frisco Bay Boy
(Rusty) is mesmerized
by handler Jane Hobson.

A cool towel helps a Bullmastiff cope with the heat of a summer show.

Handler Alan Levine baits a client.

Rusty's big win at Providence. Handler—Jane Hobson, Judge—Polly Smith.

(Photo courtesy of The Standard Image © Chuck & Sandy Tatham.)

A miniature Xoloitcuintli bitch spends most of the rare breed show held securely in her owner's loving arms.

The mostly hairless Chinese Crested dog was only recently recognized by the American Kennel Club as a member of the Toy Group. It used to be a rare breed.

Bill and Bonnie Wilson's handsome pack: Bentley of Birchmont, their German Shorthaired Pointer (at left) in the company of two Leonbergers, Koko von der Heckenrose, and her son, Aspen vom Birkenwald. (From the collection of Bill and Bonnie Wilson.)

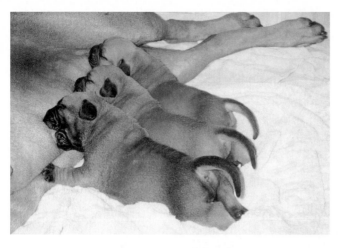

Hungry Allstar puppies at the milk bar.
(From the collection of Mimi Einstein.)

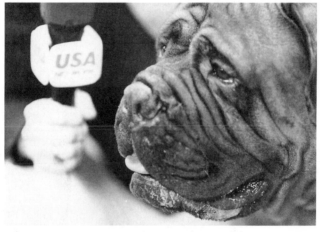

In the benching area at Madison Square Garden, the great champion Allstar's Mugsy Malone is interviewed by a television crew.

Jane Hobson commands Rusty's full attention as they compete for the Best of Breed ribbon at the Westminster Kennel Club Show.

Vito Ancona
finally finds the
puppy of his
dreams.

Retired from the
show ring to a
life of rest and
procreation,
Sam spends
many peaceful
hours by the
fireplace on his
favorite ottoman.

Jane Hobson declares when she walks in and sees that it has a slippery-nap rug on the floor rather than grippy rubber mats. The low nap and tight weave can mean trouble for big-footed dogs whose pads are smooth. 'You get a dozen of them in that ring going around, there is going to be a problem. Someone is going to take a fall."

The first to reveal the danger of the rug is a brindle puppy in the Futurity. He is a novice in the ring who for no apparent reason gets totally excited as his handler trots him in a circle; without warning, he breaks into a gallop. Spectators laugh—young dogs in this class are allowed to act silly—and the handler races forward so the puppy doesn't jerk himself against the end of the leash, but his feet want to move faster than he is able to propel himself and, like a cartoon character, his legs spin a blurred circle above the rug as he topples onto his side. Being a resilient puppy, he rights himself, uninjured, and resumes a controlled trot. Handlers are now on alert, and move their dogs around the ring with caution. Some apply a gummy commercial product called Sticky Pad to the dog's feet before entering. Others dip their dogs' feet in bowls of Coca-Cola to make them sticky. Once in the ring, though, such safety measures can wear off, so it is not uncommon to see a handler take a moment when the judge isn't watching to lick the palm of one hand and smear saliva on the pads: even a little moisture provides some grip.

In each class, once a winner has been selected the dog is led to the corner of the room where a picture is taken of the dog, its handler, its owner, and the judge. The setting for the photo is a pedestal in front of a white trellis garlanded with green plastic vines. When Darkover Beautyful In My I's takes the twelve-to-fifteen-month-old Puppy class, then Best Bitch in Futurity, she looks proud and fearless trotting around the ring. But when it comes time for the picture, the novice dog is shocked by the hollow sound her feet make when handler and co-owner Heather Silva leads her onto the pedestal. She crouches atop it, refusing to stand erect, trembling with fright—hardly the image a Bullmastiff is supposed to project. Finally, the pedestal is removed so she can pose on the solid floor and look properly fearless.

Alan Levine, outfitted in his trademark straw hat, with both ends of his white mustache perfectly curled, and wearing an especially deluxe American Indian-style belt buckle that he boasts was made from the horn of a record-breaking elk, stands on the sidelines alongside Jane Hobson. With the main events still far off, the pros observe the early Sweepstakes classes, talk shop, and trade off-color and politically incorrect jokes. And they try, in subtle or sometimes brutal ways, to throw their competition offstride and strut their toughness. To psyche out Mimi, who is a devoted activist on behalf of animal welfare, Levine brandishes his skills as a hunter. She shudders and holds her hands up to her ears. Countering his machismo, Jane Hobson flaunts her schutzhund work with Rottweilers, which involves precision control and obedience. One handler sidles up to another, commenting in a stage whisper, "I see that once again you didn't trim your nose hair for the specialty." Another woman wonders to a rival handler, "Didn't you wear that dress at the last show?"

When number 47, a big, showy pup named Lookout's Locomotion, wins the fifteen-to-eighteen-month-old Junior Dog class, murmurs of admiration sweep through the audience. The bright young animal then moves up and takes the Best of Opposite Sex ribbon in the Sweepstakes. 'You see that number forty-seven?' Levine says loud enough for all around to hear him, but leaning especially toward his rival Jane with a gloating lilt to his voice. "He's mine. I've got him next year."

"Oh, my God," Mimi says under her breath. "If he gets his hands on that dog, it is going to be big trouble."

The only time rivalries are held in check is during the contest among veteran dogs over six years old. By this stage in a Bull-mastiff's career, points and prizes are not as important as the sheer glory of competing. In most other classes, a dog is cheered only by its own faction when it gets trotted around, the hope being that the judge will be influenced by the ovation. In the veteran's ring, however, each dog receives generous applause. These oldsters, some of them with dimming eyes and scarred coats, have produced generations of champions and pets cherished by those in the room; and people cheer them out of gratitude. The hurrahs also have a poignancy, considering the relatively short lifespan of so many Bullmastiffs. Devotees of the breed who clap wildly for the veterans relish the longevity parading before them because they have all known the sorrow of losing a beloved dog at five, four, or even younger. To see an eight or nine year old in decent health is a rousing joy.

Dogs in the veteran classes are noisier than others. They pant hard after they go around the ring; their gnarled feet scrape against the rug as they try to keep up a good pace. One old brindle boy whose muscle tone gave way long ago still moves out quite well, but emits a breezy little fart with every stride.

Shastid's Spice is making her show ring debut . . . at age eleven. Known as Bea by her owners, Jack Shastid and Gerry Roach, the elderly brood bitch is a shapeless brindle thing with teats that droop to the ground and a bony head dwarfed by her spreading torso. Despite her age and the infirmities that go with it, Bea seems to be having a delightful time waiting her turn outside the ring, being sniffed and nuzzled by legions of younger dogs. When her time to be judged arrives in the class of Bitches Nine Years and Older, she is all alone in the ring. Judges usually try to appear impassive, but Charles Murphy, the judge of the Sweepstakes, cannot hide his grin of delight. Mr. Murphy is a young man who grew up raising and showing Bullmastiffs. When he sees Bea come into the ring, his eyes light up. Jack Shastid stacks her as best he can and Murphy goes through the ritual of inspecting her—teeth, head, back, hips—as her whole hindquarters wag from the attention. "Can she trot?" Murphy asks. Mr. Shastid clucks to get her attention and encourages her with all his might, as Bea moves forward and breaks into a skin-wobbling trot for a half-circle around the ring. The crowd claps with glee. As Bea slows to a more comfortable walk, judge Murphy points to her then holds his forefinger up in the air, indicating she has taken first prize . . . in her field of one.

The loudest hurrahs in the Veteran Sweepstakes are for an eight-year-old named Ladybug's Lady Caitlin T.D. Caitlin is the winningest bitch in Bullmastiff history, having taken ninety-six Best of Breed awards, including Westminster in 1993, seven Best in Shows, and two National Specialty Best of Breeds, in 1989 and 1992. Although eight, she is still fit and gorgeous. In the ring, handled by her owner, Denise Borton of Kalamazoo, Michigan, she is magical. 'What a stride!' a spectator cries out with glee as she bounds through her paces. "Look at her show!" calls another as Caitlin stops dead still for the judge, and without apparent cues from Ms. Borton, strikes a pose like a supermodel. As Mr. Murphy looks her over, she holds her noble bearing—the quintessence of vigilance and dignity, focused with utter devotion on her handler. The one other competitor in her class, Ladybug's Charlotte Wyn, is a fine-looking bitch, too; but Caitlin's charisma cannot be ignored.

Caitlin returns to the ring with all veterans that won other Sweepstakes classes, including old Bea, for the selection of Best in Veteran Sweepstakes. The judge takes his sweet time looking at the half dozen seniors circled around him, relishing their distinction, and finally tells the handlers, "I wish I could give the prize to every dog in this ring. But we all know that is not possible. So let's get it over with. Please circle around." The six dogs begin to gait around him, those too stiff to trot walking as fast as they can, as spectators rise to their feet and cheer the parade of old ones. The judge defies tradition and he himself applauds them all, beaming with his love of the breed. He then does the only thing he can do, and gives the first prize to Caitlin.

CHAPTER 9

Showdown in Plano
(Best of Breed)

Friday, Rusty is still lame. When he comes out of his room, which he shares with Jane, he surges forward with a smooth stride heading toward an appealing tree at the edge of the parking lot, but when the leash slackens, he limps. The imbalance is so negligible that an ordinary pet owner wouldn't pay it any heed if it was noticed at all. But for a dog in the National Specialty Best of Breed competition, where the goal is unblemished perfection, it is a catastrophe. Mimi and Jane hurry him along the access road a few hundred yards to the local veterinary office, where he gets a cortisone injection. He returns to the cool motel room to regain his balance in peace and quiet.

The next morning over fried eggs and coffee in the Harvey House dining room, Jane reports good news and bad news. Rusty is moving well, absolutely square. However, there is now a large lump on his back where the shot was given.

"I hope to God the vet realized that we cannot show a dog who is sound but has an obscene swelling on his back," Mimi worries. Jane reassures her that the goose egg has all day to recede before the Best of Breed event at 2:15 in the afternoon.

The big contest is being judged by Dr. Hideaki Nakazawa, a Tokyo veterinarian and Boxer breeder. He is a guest in the U.S. of the American Bullmastiff Association, which selected him because Association President Peter Aczel and some other East Coast members admire the way he has judged working breeds for the Greenwich Kennel Club. "He is a pillar of the dog fancy in Japan," Mr. Aczel boasts. "What I like best about him is that he communicates the joy of dogs in the ring. I hate a sourpuss judge who looks like someone is holding a gun to his head."

Dr. Nakazawa is a mystery to many people showing dogs in Plano. Most, including Jane and Mimi, have never seen him before and don't know what he looks like or if he speaks English; more important, they don't know if he likes stout specimens or lean ones and they cannot say—as is often said of more familiar judges—that he favors the bloodlines of one kennel over another. Back at La Guardia Airport, when Jane Hobson's carry-on bag was hand-inspected, there among her Derm Tabs for Rusty's skin and blocks of frozen chicken liver bait was a Japanese phrase book she had picked up so she could banter with the judge if the opportunity presented itself. But at the Harvey House, Dr. Nakazawa makes himself very scarce, avoiding untoward precontest socializing, lest he give the impression of favoritism. Saturday morning when a Japanese man walks past Jane in the motel hall, she flashes him a big, flirty smile, hoping he might be the judge. Mimi sees her in action, slips up close to Jane as the man walks away, apparently unimpressed, and wisecracks, "You should have lifted up your dress."

Early Saturday, Dr. Nakazawa judges Open Dogs and Open Bitches. "He looks very masculine," Jane declares when he steps into the ring for the first time. "He looks like he has a lot of testosterone." She leans toward Mimi and whispers, "Do you think I should act more American or Japanese?" The judge is a broad man in a well-tailored suit who resembles an athletic, Asian Buddy Hackett. He goes through his routine with a powerful sense of purpose as well as pleasure. Every dog is inspected in a strictly formal way; his hands move from mouth to head to shoulders, along the back and to the hindquarters quickly and confidently, never once doubling back or pausing aimlessly. He occasionally writes notes in a small book as a dog trots to and fro before him, then smiles at the handler to indicate time is up.

"I don't trust a judge who takes so many notes," Mimi grouses, sitting on the sidelines among a clutch of California breeders who are her friends. "In a big class, you can lose because of a bookkeeping error. What if he gets the numbers wrong?"

Wearing a souvenir cap she bought the previous night at the Mesquite rodeo, Jane watches the judge give the Winner's Bitch award to Beowolf Glory Girl, whose looks she doesn't like at all. "Everything just went out the window!" Jane announces to no one in particular. Turning from the ring in disgust, she spots a big male Bullmastiff someone is holding on a leash at ringside. To vent her distress and to help get her mind off the judge's decision, she starts barking, howling, and meowing in his direction. The dog, generally bored with life among the spectators, is suddenly mesmerized. "Do you want to hear my wild raccoon impression?" she asks him, then launches into a demented yodel. The dog listens so hard that he cocks his head nearly upside down with curiosity.

"I'm not with her," Mimi jokes to her colleagues, covering her face with the show's program.

The judge works so efficiently that the morning classes finish earlier than scheduled. Jane and Mimi take the free time to go to a nearby shopping mall for chicken-fried steak at a Luby's cafeteria, where they pack leftovers for Rusty. Jane, who is born-again, goes shopping in a Christian bookstore, where she finds a volume of Bible-inspired aphorisms. On the way back to the motel, she reads some aloud from the backseat of the car, explaining how each of them applies to showing dogs. " 'Nothing is accomplished without enthusiasm.' . . . 'Many people are too quick to say yes and not quick enough to say no.' That's a fact!" Jane witnesses with glee, "Like when I say, 'Yes! I can handle fifteen dogs at that show.' "

Back at the motel, Mimi holds Rusty on a leash in the parking lot while Jane comes out from her room with a choice of three outfits she can wear when she shows him: a sedate navy blue suit with wavy white piping on the collar, a royal blue dress, and a bright red suit. Wearing the black military-style boots she prefers for casual attire and no stockings, Jane throws on each of the outfits just to check the fit. She likes the navy one best, but Mimi decides she hates it, declaring, "If we lose, it's because you chose the wrong dress."

"What does the ass look like?" Jane asks. "Is it too bulky? Do the thighs look thunderous?"

Jane runs back and forth in the parking lot with Rusty to see how the dress looks in action, as it will look when she takes him around the ring. They agree it is too drab. Jane then tries the red suit. "No! The color clashes with Rusty and the shoulders are so big they will make his look small," Mimi says.

Jane holds the royal blue dress on a hanger, waving it in front of Rusty's face, meowing and yelping to perk his interest. "Uh-oh, he is looking at my hairy legs," Jane says.

"That's all right, he's got a hairy face," Mimi answers.

After resolving she will wear the royal blue, Jane concocts a mixture of Coca-Cola and extra sugar in a metal dish and sets it on top of the hood of the car in the parking lot, where it can cook in the sun and then be used as a dip to give Rusty's feet traction. When it warms up, Mimi takes it to the ballroom where the competition will take place and Jane returns with Rusty to their room to get ready.

At 2 P.M., fifteen minutes before Best of Breed judging is to begin, Jane is outfitted in the blue dress with clean white sneakers on her feet and pantyhose on her newly shaven legs. It is time to take Rusty for his walk. She leads him down the road behind the motel and into a scrubby lot behind a Taylor Rental store. Along the way, he pees a dozen times, sniffs every rock and tree, and finally finds a pleasant place to squat behind an abandoned school bus, named TEEN MACHINE, from the Meadows Baptist Church of Plano. "He's not acting too normal, if you ask me," Jane says with some dismay, groaning when she notes that his stool isn't as firm as she would like it to be. Back in the room, she grabs a mass of paper towels and wipes his hind end, exclaiming, "You smell like a diarrhea dog!" She then takes out a stick of grooming chalk to touch up a few spots where his red coat is scuffed.

It is critical that Rusty be a hundred percent alert when he enters the ring so that he grabs the attention of the judge. To achieve this state of mind in a breed of animal who is so fundamentally unflappable, Jane has brought her prong collar, a chain-link neckpiece with dull metal points that provokes a dog's full attention when it is yanked. The collar, however, was recently used on one of her schutzhund Rottweilers, for whom she had to remove several links; so it no longer fits around Rusty's giant neck. "I'll just have to use my strong arms," she tells him as she puts a regular choke chain around his neck and gives him two or three sharp corrections. His eyes open wide. She gets down on her knees and stares hard into his eyes, nose to nose—a posture sure to stir the competitive juices in any healthy male dog. "Are you ready to show?" she shouts into his face like a marine drill instructor. He gleams at her, tongue wagging. She stands and wipes a moist towel along his back, then stands over him, astraddle. She slaps both his sides hard, calling out "I said, *are you ready to show?!*" His tail is wagging fast. He wants to pounce somewhere.

When Jane opens the motel room door, Rusty storms out

from between her legs. She runs behind him at top speed, holding the other end of his leash. Like a low-flying cruise missile, the charging Bullmastiff causes shocked guests to hug the wall when they hear him gallop up behind; they then gape in awe as he and Jane disappear ahead.

Rusty and Jane arrive just at 2:15 outside the joined meeting rooms Trinity II and III, where the hallway is thronged with sixty other competitors, each of them honed to peak condition. The smell of nerves and sweat in the air is more human than canine, but it puts the dogs on edge, for their olfactory powers are tremendous. There isn't a scuffle among them—an amazing situation, considering five dozen finely tuned bruisers are crowded into such a small area, some practically on top of others. But being Bullmastiffs—working dogs, bred to guard rather than to fight—all their nervous energy gets focused on the job at hand, embodied in the person who holds their leash. It is impressive to see all the wrinkled brows and rock-steady postures, each dog waiting for a cue to do what he or she has been trained to do.

The anxious handlers share one fashion in common—ground-gripping shoes so they can run alongside the animal they are showing; but otherwise, they are tremendously diverse in style and physique. There are big bulky ones whose bodies flap like old elephants when they traverse the ring looming over their dogs; there are swift, frosted-blonde gazelles whose svelte frames make their dogs look all the beefier; there are pudgy men in tight jackets outgrown a decade ago and trim women in dress-for-success suits; there are mannish spinsters in tweed, prim matrons in 1950s polka dots, and breeders' kids in their Sunday best like Brylcreemed 4-H competitors with prize swine.

"Oh, my, look at us—we're in a tux," Barbara Heck says out loud when the judge enters the room dressed in formal wear for the contest. Her champion Sunny—Briart's Solar Power—stands regally at her feet.

"Maybe he's trying out for a job as headwaiter," another handler pipes up under his breath, trying to break the tension with impertinence as he straightens the knot in his necktie.

Each of the sixty handlers has a Bullmastiff at he end of a leash, but considering there is a breed standard and that each dog became a champion because it fit that standard, the variety among this one breed is astonishing, nearly as wide as that among the people showing them. When Dr. Nakazawa calls all competitors into the ring so he can see the entire field, sixty dogs form three concentric circles around the perimeter. Some, like Rusty, are brawny athletes; a few are even bigger—so grotesquely oversized they seem like glandular oddities. A handful have legs like stilts and long muzzles that appear to have been borrowed from a sporting hound; and a couple of low-slung specimens sport toothy faces that are nearly Bulldog-flat.

Each dog has a number, and because they are called into the ring in order, Jane finds herself and Rusty (number 149) right behind Norma Gibson, who is handling Leatherneck's Bit of Happylegs (number 147). Bit is one of the top-winning Bullmastiffs in the country, and Miss Gibson—a tall blonde in a bright yellow suit—is known as a deadly serious handler who doesn't cut her competition any slack. But as the judge looks around at the assembled dogs, Jane takes the initiative. While baiting Rusty with pieces of liver, she happens to throw some in the direction of Bit, causing him to momentarily lose his focus on Miss Gibson.

"Let's make a pact," she says to Jane in an ominous tone. "Don't crowd me . . . *and I won't crowd you.*"

"If you didn't use ten-year-old liver, your dog wouldn't be so distractible," Jane answers, unfazed.

Having seen them all together, the judge sends all the dogs

out of the ring, then divides them into six groups—three sets of males, three sets of females—so he can call them back to be inspected in manageable bunches.

When Jane's group is called she skips into the ring with a tremendous wad of moist white chicken meat half-sticking out of her mouth: Rusty's bait. Dr. Nakazawa puts Rusty through the exact routine he uses on each and every other dog—quickly inspecting the mouth, head, shoulders, back, and hindquarters, then sending him on a diagonal trot back and forth. Jane fears he doesn't take enough notes as he watches her move around the ring. Is this a sign that he might not think Rusty worthy of surviving the first cut? Furthermore, Jane is rattled by something she sees: While stacking Rusty for inspection, she glances to the sidelines, where Sherri Samel, a well-known handler from Texas, is leaning over Mimi's chair, deep in some kind of conference. Mimi later tells Jane that Sherri was complimenting Rusty, but at that moment, when all her attention is needed to present Rusty to the judge, Jane wonders, *Is Sherri giving Mimi a critique of my handling techniques?*

Panting harder than Rusty, her face red from the tension of her few moments with Dr. Nakazawa, Jane hurried out of the ring, full of doubts and second thoughts. "See that girl in the tight dress with the big ass?" she says of another handler she just went against. "He looked at her more than me. I knew I should have worn red."

By 4 P.M., every dog in the contest has come and gone before the judge and he is preparing to announce his first cut. He stands in the center of the ring, now empty of all dogs, conferring with the ring steward. Around them, the ballroom is filled to maximum capacity. There is no fixed rule for winnowing down a very large field. A judge might excuse half the dogs before he reinspects the other half, or he could cut just one-third of them, then a portion of those that remain, before he does his final judging.

Most people assume that from a field of sixty dogs this good, at least a couple dozen will get called back into the ring. The steward steps to a microphone to read the numbers of those who have made the cut, inviting them to return so they can now be measured against one another for the top prize. Astoundingly, he calls out a mere twelve numbers. Dr. Nakazawa has narrowed down the field that fast, without a second look at the other forty-eight. His choices include Alan Levine and Ladybug Thorn of the Rose B.D., Norma Gibson and Leatherneck's Bit of Happylegs, and Sherri Samel who is handling Mr. U's Music Man, the only Bullmastiff ever to win the Working Group at the Westminster Kennel Club show in New York. Mr. U's Music Man, known as Satch, is eight years old, but still vibrant; and in the hands of Miss Samel, who took him to the heights at Madison Square Garden in 1993, he is the epitome of canine showmanship. To the bewilderment of many, Ladybug's Lady Caitlin is among the dogs excused from competition.

Rusty is another one the judge no longer wants to see. At 4:15, Jane races back through the halls of the motel room toward their room with Rusty still charging forward, full of competitive energy. But for him and for Jane, the contest is over.

It is an education to behold Sherri Samel work the veteran Satch in the ring. When the judge looks their way, the big red dog is statuesque—head perked, eyes focused, on his toes; and Sherri, a pretty blonde with hawk eyes and a lean-muscled body, radiates confidence. "She is the female Alan Levine," Mimi says. "But she does it with style and grace." To an untrained eye, she doesn't appear to be working hard when she stacks Satch or runs with him or kneels in front of him to provoke an expression of perfect vigilance. But the sight lines between her and the dog never weaken; she keeps his attention locked onto her in such a way that the two of them become an inseparable unit, as tightly synchronized as ballroom dancers in a sinewy tango. On two occasions, when the judge takes considerable time looking at another of the finalists, Sherri somehow coaxes Satch to issue a bark: psychological warfare. It isn't a loud or rude bark; in fact it is so quick and subtle that unless you are listening for it, your conscious mind might not notice it at all. The judge himself pays no overt attention to the subliminal distraction; and yet, each time Satch barks, Dr. Nakazawa's focus on the other dog is momentarily snapped.

Except for a few squalling human babies, the ballroom is hushed as the twelve finalists are gone over. Alan Levine steps back from Thorn, allowing the winningest Bullmastiff in the country to stand for inspection without any baiting or coaxing. Mimi mutters, "Oh, God, no, please, no." But when Dr. Nakazawa sends Mimi's arch-nemesis to the front of the line, then tells him to lead the rest of the dogs in one final circle around, a roar of joy goes up from Thorn's camp on the sidelines. He has won. The judge points his forefinger at Alan Levine and Thorn, anointing their status as the best handler and best Bullmastiff in America.

At ringside, Mimi looks like a locomotive ran over her. Recalling Rusty's wins over Thorn earlier in the season, she says with limp enthusiasm: "We can now advertise that we are one of the few dogs to have beaten the national specialty Best of Breed winner." It is inconceivable to her that Dr. Nakazawa made his choice without prejudice. Like many breeders who don't take the big prize, Mimi rationalizes the loss by demonizing the judge that chose her rival. "I can tell you this," she announces to her coterie of friends. "That judge did his homework. He read the journals, he saw the big advertisements, he learned who's who. I say he made up his mind before he got on the plane in Japan."

Ed Silva, whose daughter Heather and their handsome dog

Sherwood's Jacob were among the forty-eight who didn't make the first cut, comes close to Mimi and declares, "We could have hired an American judge who would have done the same effin' thing, for much less money. And it was a disgrace for Caitlin to be ignored." To Heather, he says, "C'mon, let's go congratulate Alan Levine. I want to vomit on his tie, but we'll shake his hand."

"Alan Levine will now be impossible to beat," Barbara Heck says. "He has so much momentum that he'll be going in and out of Best of Breed classes all by himself. Who dares go against him now? Everybody else is going to pull in their horns. The only thing we can do is buy a trailer and move to a different part of the country. I am happy for Alan, though. He was so fond of Thorn's mother, Angelica Rose. They had a special relationship. It means a lot for him to take the national specialty with her son."

"Do you realize what we are up against now?" Mimi groans later that afternoon over drinks in the motel lobby bar.

Without warning, Mimi stands up and leaves her friends in the bar, vanishing into the hallway for fifteen minutes. She returns, suddenly full of fire, and whispers to them, "Listen, and listen well. Sherri Samel is leaving with her van in an hour for a show in Tyler, Texas. She likes Rusty and she wants to handle him, and I think the two of them could be unstoppable. I have to decide right now if I want to turn him over to her. She would campaign him full guns in the Southwest, and she can win. "As Mimi speaks, she gazes across the bar to Jane Hobson, who is drinking margaritas with some fellow handlers. "Sherri is a hot number, out for blood, and she is well-enough connected to break him out of the breed. Rusty's two big group wins this year have been under old-time judges who don't give a damn about advertisements and connections and have the confidence to put up the best dog, regardless of Thorn's hype. The problem is that there aren't enough judges like that; and now Alan Levine has the East locked up. Back there, Rusty doesn't have a chance. The only shot he has is for me to leave him here in Texas with Sherri."

Mimi fires up a cigarette, girds herself with a deep drag, and walks over to Jane. She pulls her aside and asks her what she thinks Rusty's chances would be if Sherri Samel handled him. Jane is not completely stunned. She has felt as frustrated as Mimi trying to beat Alan Levine, and she voices some relief that she will no longer have to battle the Unbeatable One. Pretending to be happy, she announces she is thrilled to be able to devote all her attention now to her Rottweilers. She then excuses herself and goes back to her motel room alone at a quick trot.

An hour later, Sherri Samel and Mimi go to get Rusty, who is still with Jane. They knock on Jane's door. Inside, Jane's voice can be heard, theatrically loud: "You'll love her, Rusty, you'll just love her." Declaring the room too messy, Jane squeezes out the door to talk in the hallway. Her hair is soaking wet, plastered to her head from a quick swim in the motel pool. Although they have competed in the ring, Jane and Sherri have never been formally introduced. They say hello, then the three women discuss a hundred details in the short time Sherri has before leaving: Rusty's diet (lamb and rice), his daily lecithin (from the health food store), his Derm Tabs for dry skin ("I use those on my dogs every day," Sherri says), parvo shots, last blood work.

"I would like to take him to Dr. Johnston, the vet I use," Sherri says. "He is incredible. Expensive, but the best." In the flurry of the sudden decision, Mimi has not discussed costs or price at all with Sherri.

"He has had all his shots?" Sherri asks. "I need his rabies papers. Texas is under a quarantine." As Mimi goes to her room, next door, to get the papers, Sherri and Jane look each other over. Finally Jane says, "I'll go get him," and retreats into her room. She comes out with Rusty at the end of a lead line.

"Do you like his weight?" Sherri asks Mimi.

"I could see another pound on him," Mimi says.

Sherri says, "I like him as he is." Jane agrees that he is just right.

"He can take a correction," Jane tells Sherri. "He needs it to stand still. I use the prong collar before a show. . . . He is great, but he is horrendous with toes and whiskers. Trimming him can be dangerous."

Sherri bends down and hugs and kisses Rusty in a gesture of welcome. Although she is a mighty competitor in the show ring, she is a small, slender woman; and the contrast between her and the husky dog, who appears to outweigh her by at least thirty pounds, is dramatic.

When Mimi tells her about his cortisone injection the day before, Sherri looks him in the eyes, affectionately grasping both sides of his enormous face by the jowls, and says in a sweet feminine voice, "Well, then, Rusty, you'll need to tee-tee more than usual today."

"He adapts to everyone," Jane says as she moves aside to let Sherri play with her former ward. "He is excellent with other dogs. He is unbelievable with puppies, bitches, and strangers."

"I think the key is to have him around me, just hanging around for a while," Sherri tells Mimi. The trial period is inevitable anyway, because entries close three weeks before each show, meaning she will have him that long before she can begin to take him on the Southwest circuit.

"I condition him a mile on my bicycle every day, but on soft ground, not cement," Jane says. "He needs to work or he doesn't eat. No exercise, no appetite."

"Good," says Sherri. "I'll ride with him using a leather leash, five days a week."

Jane bends down to give Rusty a final hug around his neck. She kisses his wet nose and lingers there, face to face, as Rusty's hot breath washes over her for the last time. His eyes are shining; his toothy smile goes ear to ear. Sherri gathers the collar around his neck, preparing to leave.

Sherri leads Rusty away. "It's the changing of the guard, the changing of the guard," Jane mutters to herself before receding into the motel room.

As Sherri goes to pull her van around, Mimi takes Rusty for a final walk along the motel grass exercise area among some trees. He lifts his leg, kicks some turf, then stops his exploration to look up at her, wondering where they are going next. "It's so sudden, so fast," she says to him, patting his broad head.

Sherri's immaculate van contains three large dog crates, water bottles, collars, leashes, and other show paraphernalia lined up as neatly as equipment in an ambulance. She calls Rusty to the side door, where he hops up and agreeably walks into the open crate she has for him. "Rusty, have you ever been to Tyler, Texas?" Sherri asks as she climbs forward to sit behind the wheel. "It's a very pretty town." It is dusk when she pulls onto the highway heading for the next dog show, with her new client looking out through the bars of his crate on the van floor behind her.

That night in the Harvey House motel ballroom, the American Bullmastiff Association holds its banquet. Because it's Texas and so many people are from elsewhere, a cowboy theme was chosen months ago when the event was planned. The meal is barbecued brisket and beans; decor is cowboy-western, too, including centerpieces on the table that cause breeders and handlers to gasp with some dismay and a measure of amusement: Every table is arranged around a straw Stetson like the one Alan Levine always wears.

CHAPTER 10

Leonberger
Love Connection

Bill and Bonnie Wilson are perfectionists who are rather per-
fect-looking themselves. She is a diminutive blonde with a
button nose and a tiny dress size to match—so elfin that when
she was a first-class Pan Am stewardess some years ago, she
easily took her catnaps in the luggage bins above the seats
when the plane was empty. Bill is tall, square-jawed, Ivy
League handsome, and a top executive with a computer company outside Boston. Their bright yellow house in Sudbury is
called "The Ivy." It looks like a country inn—so handsome
that passers-by sometimes stop along the road to gape or take
a picture, no doubt thinking it's a famous landmark. Inside,
room after room is filed with precious treasures from their
years of traveling the globe separately and together. Carpets
bear the symmetrical vacuum marks of perfect housekeeping;
the master bedroom, where the canopy bed is draped in yards
of gauzy fabric, leads directly to an immense indoor swimming pool. The Wilsons are known among their friends for
their spectacular Christmas parties, which they hold every few
years rather than annually because one year is not enough
time to plan the kind of affair they like to host—to find the
perfect tree, hire the perfect caterer, and select perfect holiday
decor.

The Wilsons, who have no children, got their first dog, a German Short-haired Pointer, the week after their honeymoon. They have had German Short-haired Pointers since then; their current one, Bentley of Birchmont, holds three behavior and obedience degrees: T.T. (for "temperament tested"), C.G.C. ("canine good citizen"), and C.D.X. ("companion dog excellent"). Bentley is a tidy fellow who scarcely leaves pawprints when he glides across the thick carpet of the Wilsons' home. Bill always wanted a really big dog, but they resisted getting one because most of the big ones drool too much. Then in 1990 something happened that changed their lives and, at the same time, altered the fate of a breed.

Bill and Bonnie were vacationing in the south of France, one of a handful of places on their well-researched list of possibilities for a perfect retirement in the not too distant future. "We were strolling through Nîmes along a quaint cobblestone street," Bonnie recalls. "Out of a butcher shop bounded this one-hundred-fifty-pound male dog. There was a little Dachshund outside, too. We watched as the big dog lay down and the puppy climbed all over it and they played." Impressed by the big dog's easy-going temperament, the Wilsons asked the butcher what breed it was. He told them it was a Leonberger.

Developed in Germany in the 1840s by breeding Newfoundlands to Saint Bernards, a Leonberger looks like a cross between a dog and a lion. It was never extremely popular even in Europe, where the breed nearly died out as a result of World War Two; it was unheard of in the U.S. until a few were imported in the 1970s, and the American Kennel Club still does not recognize it. But the Wilson's encounter was magical. "The romance of discovering this dog on a cobblestone street in Nîmes possessed me," Bonnie says. "The minute we got back to the U.S. I started calling all the dog people I could find, but nobody knew anything about Leonbergers. Finally, after much detective work, I got in touch with a woman who was breeding them in Illinois, one of five breeders in the country at the time."

Sylvia Kaufmann proved to be as scrupulous as the Wilsons. "She was not at all eager to grab us as customers," Bonnie recalls. "But I called and wrote her constantly in hopes that we would become her favorite people. Lucky for us, her bitch was about to whelp." After weeks of correspondence, Sylvia agreed to sell the Wilsons a puppy. Once the litter was born, Bonnie mailed her an intricate "Puppy Test" she had found in a magazine, which promised to determine which dog in a litter had the best personality. Bonnie did not want merely a droolless dog: "I wanted a dog that would look up at me lovingly and say, 'You're the greatest thing since sliced bread!' "

When the pups were eight weeks old and ready for their new homes, Bill flew to Chicago and drove out to the kennel at seven in the morning. "I wanted to be first in line," he says with the determination and confidence of someone who has climbed to the top of the corporate ladder. He was offered two puppies from which to choose—the ones that had passed the test Bonnie had sent. He picked up the one that was taller and wrote a check for $750.

When Bill arrived home with Koko von der Heckenrose, Bonnie was ecstatic. The puppy was affectionate and sweet: a perfect pet. At the time, a pet was all they wanted. "We had no intention of showing or breeding dogs," Bonnie says, "but we were so interested in them, and we knew so little about them, that when we heard that there was going to be a Leonberger specialty show in Baltimore that year, we felt we had to go. After everything we had gone through to get Koko, we already felt we were part of the Leonberger crowd." The Wilsons took Koko with them and met forty other dogs and their owners. Koko was just four months old at the time and, like all beautiful babies, she was swooned over and kootchy-kooed, which Bonnie relished. "I wanted everyone to think she was the most beautiful dog with the best temperament, just the best dog ever," Bonnie remembers.

Someone convinced Bonnie and Bill to enter Koko in the young puppy judging, so Bonnie borrowed a show leash and led her into the ring. "I had absolutely no idea what I was doing. I pushed her stomach up so high her back arched like a mountain. Even so, she won her class. We then came back for the selection of Best Puppy, which included dogs up to eighteen months old, and she won again! I got a trophy and a ribbon and I thought, *this is really fun.*"

A short time later, the American Rare Breed Association (ARBA) held its first national show in Washington, D.C. The Wilsons brought Koko and she won Best of Breed ribbons under four separate judges. Photographs of Koko's wins that weekend show Bonnie holding her in show position for the camera, alongside the judge. They are the standard winner's shot taken after the judging at every dog show, but Bonnie does not look like a standard handler. She has an infectious smile on her face, she wears a variety of stylish dresses in the different pictures, and her hair is flawlessly coiffed. She is the only handler we have ever seen in a show ring picture who is as nicely posed and groomed as the dog being shown.

Before too long the Leonberger Club of America needed a new secretary. Bonnie volunteered and launched into the job with gusto. The more she learned about Koko and her kind, the more she felt the urge to do something to help and protect the breed. The best way to do that, of course, is to create more of them. She and Bill thought it might be fun to raise a litter of puppies.

For the Wilsons, the decision to breed was not a casual one.

It was made with a sense of duty—to ensure all the qualities of the Leonberger they liked so much—including not only its leonine appearance, but also its extraordinarily gentle disposition and its innate sociability. When Koko was two, they began the search for her Mr. Right with all the earnestness of a royal family seeking out a consort for a queen. "There are so few dogs, you need to be careful," Bonnie explains. "The gene pool is small, and that makes every breeding count."

When they determined there were no acceptable canine suitors in the United States, the Wilsons figured that the Leonberger of their dreams might be found in the dog's ancestral homeland. They flew to Germany and drove to the village of Leonberg, where 150 years ago Mayor Heinrich Essig had first conceived the breed to resemble the town's crest, a lion. "We expected to see Leonbergers all over the place," Bonnie recalls. "But we did not see one. Many people there didn't even know what we were talking about when we said the name of the dog." The Wilsons did finally locate some nice-looking German specimens, but they did not pass muster because they suffered from hip dysplasia, a painful affliction dogs pass down to their offspring. Discouraged, the couple flew back to the United States to break the news to Koko that she was to remain a maiden.

Bonnie heard about a Leonberger in England who had taken Best of Breed the previous year at Crufts, the world's largest dog show. His name was Leonberget'z Crusader from Atlantis at Manorguard—Jabba for short—and he was a Swedish import. Thoughts of Jabba's perfection made the Wilsons' hopes soar with the anticipation of a potential love connection, but because taking Koko to him would require putting her in quarantine for six months according to British dog-import laws, they began to research artificial insemination. Outside of Philadelphia, they found a biologist named

George Govette who said he could do the job. Mr. Govette so impressed them with his confidence that the Wilsons began referring to him as The Inseminator, in homage to Arnold Schwartzenegger's movie, *The Terminator.*

To make sure Jabba was their boy, Bonnie flew to Birmingham to the next Crufts show. "I was jet-lagged and exhausted, racing toward the ring where the Leonbergers were being shown. And there was this big, wonderful dog lying on his back getting his toenails clipped in preparation for the ring. I asked, 'Is this Jabba?' You know what? He was."

Alas, Jabba was not perfect. "His mask was not as dark as Koko's," Bonnie remembers. "His front feet turned out a little, too." Nevertheless, he was a beauty. "His topline was like a board, he had big bones, a great rear, and movement to die for." Convinced she had found what she was looking for, she made arrangements with Jabba's owner. She then sent word to The Inseminator, who flew to England to collect semen from the dog. The Wilsons later jumped for joy when Mr. Govette called to tell them that Jabba's sperm had good motility. They bought the entire cover of the American Leonberger Club's quarterly *LeoLetter* for Spring 1993 and printed a picture of Jabba on the lower right side of the page, gazing upward longingly. Above him was a lover's heart and a dreamy thought balloon showing Koko looking down at him in rapture.

Late that winter, with Koko on the verge of coming into season, the northeastern United States was hit by a devastating blizzard the press labeled "The Storm of the Century." Power went out; highways closed; everything stopped . . . except for Bonnie Wilson, who piled in her Blazer with Koko and drove to Philadelphia, where Jabba's frozen semen awaited. "The plan was for me to check in at some No-tell Motel on the outskirts of the city. I was to stay there with

Koko. Every day, we met with George so he could perform tests to see if she was ready. I was a nervous wreck but Koko took it like a champ. Finally the moment arrived. He inseminated her twice, holding her upside down for five minutes after each time."

Koko was the first Leonberger to be artificially inseminated, and she also turned out to be the first American dog of any breed to produce a live litter from frozen European semen. Sixty-three days after conception, she gave birth to twelve puppies. One was stillborn, another died a week later; but the rest survived. Ten healthy, well-bred Leonbergers joined the world's population.

For three weeks, Bill and Bonnie Wilson slept alongside Koko and her litter, taking turns staying awake to watch the cherished little ones. They started a photo album of the blessed event, including pictures of Koko and the puppies frolicking in their hand-painted whelping box. They took individual portraits of each of the puppies, every one identified by a collar made of different-colored rickrack. Nearby in each photo is a pack of Marlboros so you can see how small the dog is. Following the puppy pictures in the album are pictures subsequently sent to the Wilsons by the people to whom they sold the puppies. They show a blissful world of happy adoptees. There is a Leonberger in a Santa Claus outfit next to a Christmas tree, there are Leonbergers playing in backyards with children, there is one Leonberger who became a search-and-rescue dog outside Hartford, Connecticut. "He is the only one on his team that does cadavers. All the other dogs are scared to sniff them out," Bonnie boasts.

Jabba has never met his American children, but Bonnie Wilson knows he is happy. She says that when the stud dog saw George Govette at Crufts the following year, he went galloping over to him and jumped up, laying both paws on the man's shoulders. "I guess he liked the way George collected the semen," Bonnie chirps.

She is now looking for a suitable mate for the son of Koko that she kept, Aspen vom Birkenwald. She has heard there is a beautiful bitch just right for him who lives in Italy.

CHAPTER 11

Rusty Come Home

Few show dogs are able to balance a full home life with a successful career. Most competitors on the circuit live like rodeo's gypsy cowboys: constantly on the move from one contest to the next in their year-round quest for glory. So it has been for Rusty, a dog who has never known what it is like to chase squirrels across a lawn in his own backyard or to spend idle days on the couch in the den, watching TV with the family. He is a beautiful Bullmastiff with a happy-go-lucky personality, and thanks to Jane Hobson's daily regimen of jogging and exercise, he is in tip-top shape. And yet he has not been able to deliver on his promise of greatness in the ring.

Mimi hoped that after his shunning by Dr. Nakazawa at the specialty, Rusty would blaze a new trail of success throughout the Southwest, winning group placements and perhaps even a best in show. But two months later, hopes are fading. Handler Sherri Samel seems unable to do better with him than Jane Hobson had done back East; Rusty is winning Best of Breed competitions, but hasn't yet won the Working Group.

Mimi is particularly troubled that she has received no photographs of Rusty and Sherri with his blue ribbons, a fact Sherri explains by saying that he won't behave well enough to pose for the pictures. The pictures themselves don't matter much (although Mimi needs them if she is going to place advertisements in the dog show journals—an important component of a winning campaign). What worries her is the relationship of Rusty and Sherri. Is he too much dog for her? Is Jane Hobson—tall and muscular and with a dominant personality that has set her in good stead training Schutzhund dogs—the only person who can show Rusty to best advantage? When she had him at the end of her leash, he displayed all his vigor, but he was also totally under her control, as must be the case with any dog in the ring, large or small.

Is Rusty simply too much dog? It is a question Mimi herself sometimes ponders. "I really don't like him," she blurts out one day, then instantly feels guilty. "I mean, I do like Rusty; he is wonderful, really wonderful," she says, explaining that she often feels the need to toughen her feelings about a dog she actually likes very much, but sees so little because of all the time he spends on the show circuit. Hers is a dilemma felt by the loved ones of many great athletes: She wants Rusty to achieve his maximum potential in the ring, which means months away from home, and yet she also wants him for herself.

Mimi is also aware that Rusty's high energy personality, which makes him show so well, limits his future potential as a house pet, except in the home of a dog lover willing to live with a boisterous creature trained to assert his status as top dog. As Mimi considers his fate, she begins to worry that Rusty is like a pugilist who has trained all his life to fight, knows nothing else, and yet now must face the fact that he may never win the world. What do you do with a character like that?

Mimi uses Rusty's assertive personality as an example of her most dreaded moments as a breeder: when someone to whom she has sold a dog calls her a year and a half later to say, "My big male dog will not get off the bed, and when I try to make him move, he growls at me. What should I do?"

"How can I tell such a person that by the time they call me

it is too late?" Mimi says. She explains that the problem is that Bullmastiff puppies are adorable tubby teddy bears, so much so that many novice owners let them get away with what seems like harmless mischief. It can be delightful to see a bright-eyed, eight-week-old puppy wrestle a pillow off a chair; but when a one-hundred-sixty-pound whirling dervish pulls a living room couch around the room, shredding cushions and snapping wood with glee, it ain't so cute anymore. And then the phone calls start. Although Rusty is no miscreant, his problem is that the people who owned him during his first year weren't strict enough. He never really learned the fundamental lesson, that he must behave. "Jane can handle him well because Jane is really, really tough," Mimi says. "She has the attitude: *obey or else!* Any handler who does not dominate Rusty with absolute conviction has no chance with him. A dog like him will take advantage of what he knows and pretty soon you'll be the one at the end of the leash, and he'll be calling all the shots."

With Rusty not pulling in the big wins, Mimi must now rethink his career and his future. Two solutions present themselves: A wealthy man from Oklahoma has expressed interest in buying him and taking over his show career. "Sometimes the best thing that can happen to a breeder is for someone with a serious amount of time and money to buy your dog and campaign him," Mimi says, considering Rusty's fate. If someone else takes responsibility for his career, he would still be an Allstar dog, so Mimi's kennel would receive the glory of his victories; but the new owner would pay the showing and handling fees and transportation, all of which easily can reach $100,000 a year for a serious campaign. That much money is far more than Mimi spends campaigning a dog, although the expenses do add up. When asked how much money can be made breeding show dogs, Mimi's husband Arthur once joked, "I have to wait until Mimi gives up her dog business before I can afford to retire."

Another possibility for Rusty's future is a prominent African-American lawyer from the deep South who saw Rusty being shown by Sherri and was so impressed that he decided he needs to own an Allstar dog himself. The lawyer, who has a wife and small children, has launched a serious letter-writing, fax, and phone crusade imploring Mimi to sell him one. Like a lovestruck suitor, the lawyer declares his honorable intentions of providing any Allstar dog he gets with a home worthy of a prince, and laying out his credentials for dog ownership to Mimi in such a way that in any nondog context he would be considered a fantastic catch: successful, rich, connected, and powerful in his community. He wants a puppy; but it was Rusty who won his heart. Perhaps, Mimi wonders, he would be happy with Rusty himself *and* a puppy.

Mimi is tempted by the offers and possibilities, but instinct tells her to play Rusty close to her chest. Still, it is a real dilemma to figure out exactly what to do with him. Young, beautiful, charming, and a potent champion, he is neither an ideal pet nor has he established himself in the show ring the way Mimi feels he can. The wealthy Oklahoman and the southern lawyer are both possibilities, but Mimi isn't certain either man would know how to tap the show ring potential she believes Rusty has. And yet, Sherri Samel—whose skills as a handler are above reproach—has not been able to break him out, either.

"Rusty is a very nice dog," Mimi says, contemplating his career. "A real show dog, with the kind of energy it takes to win. On a good day, he can knock off anybody, and he *has* beaten them all, including Thorn, when the judge gives him a fair shake. But I have no illusions. Rusty is no Martin and he is no Mugsy (the two greatest Allstar champions); I just don't know if he can be a superstar." For now, Mimi decides to keep him in Texas with Sherri. Her contact with Rusty is dim. She gets some ribbons in the mail along with Sherri's bills. He is out of sight; some days, he is even out of mind. But the holding pattern is snapped late in November.

"I can win with Rusty!" Jane Hobson says to Mimi. "I know I can win with him. Please bring him back."

Since losing Rusty after the Dallas Specialty, Jane has remained central in Mimi's life, working with two Allstar dogs. One, Sonny Boy (a.k.a. Son of Sam), has outgrown his awkward phase and shows tremendous promise. But he is still not yet mature enough to campaign. "He is a wild thing!" Mimi declares with pride early in 1996. "He is very big, structurally correct with a level topline and a good bite, but his head needs to broaden and his rear is still immature, not yet square. He is just about the happiest dog I've ever seen, tail banging into everything all the time. Jane gives him a hard correction, and he smiles and wags at her." The plan is to introduce Sonny Boy to the show world at the next East Coast Weekend in May.

Jane has also taken possession once again of another of Mimi's dogs, the illustrious Allstar's Nathan Detroit (Ned), who retired from the show ring after dazzling the dog fancy by taking Best of Breed at the Westminster Kennel Club show in Madison Square Garden in 1994. Ned's career was incredibly short—one glamorous season with Jane, ending at the summit of the show world in February at the Garden, after which he retired to a life of stud service. And now, with the 1996 Westminster Kennel Club show on the horizon, and Rusty's future iffy, Mimi is desperate to field a great Allstar dog in the most prestigious of shows. If Ned is sound, and if Jane can once again fire up his competitive spirit, it would be a dramatic comeback for him to appear in the ring at the Garden, two years after his sensational win. This is similar to the plan Mimi had for Sam that was sidetracked by his lackadaisical attitude. Perhaps it could work for Ned, who as a stud living in the kennel has never had Sam's opportunity to succumb to the sybaritic pleasures of being a house dog.

The field at the Westminster Kennel Club show is limited to 2,500 dogs, all champions. Mimi enters Ned as well as Rusty, and it is Jane's task to get Ned back into show shape. But like Sam, he has a bad knee; and although a careful conditioning program is planned to overcome the weakness, several weeks of cautious exercise only exacerbate the problem. Ned returns to Mimi's Katonah kennel in January with a limp. "He'll not make the Garden," Mimi declares. It would be humiliating to bring her champion back into that ring if he is even a little bit off. So the entry is wasted and Mimi's hopes for a great Allstar showing at Westminster now fall entirely onto Rusty's beefy shoulders.

Jane desperately tries to convince Mimi that she and Rusty can now beat Alan Levine and Thorn. Wishful rumors have spread in the Bullmastiff world that the Garden might be Thorn's last show. The enduring champion, now six years old, is supposedly ready to retire. He is the consummate pro, and he has regularly won breed and group placements since his big victory in Dallas, and during the winter months he takes two back-to-back Best In Show awards in upstate New York. But those who handle Thorn's rivals are now speculating that his best days are behind him. Jane has watched him in the winter East Coast shows, and she attributes his continuing success only to momentum and to the fact that his relentless winning streak scares away any serious competitors. She is confident that a young, explosive dog—a dog just like Rusty, handled with the right panache—could knock off Thorn even before the Garden. With the smell of victory in her nostrils, Jane calls Mimi and pleads, "I want my dog back!"

In January, Rusty returns. Mimi worries that he has lost some weight while in Texas—no dog is ever quite big enough to suit her—but Jane thinks he looks fine. After Jane picks him up at Newark airport, Rusty leaps from his crate, positively thrilled. He rears back, lunges forward, and wraps his front legs around her thighs, hugging her with glee until Jane barks at him in her most ferocious dog-trainer voice. "It took him a while to remember who I am," she says. "He is so overexcited to be back home." Mimi worries about his wild behavior, but Jane is unfazed by the one-hundred-thirty-five-pound reprobate now living in her house whom she has to prepare for Madison Square Garden in less than a month. In truth, Jane relishes Rusty's assertive canine personality, not just because she likes lively dogs. In the show ring, that kind of exuberance can win ribbons.

"It's like starting an old relationship again," she says, watching Rusty pad about, sniffing familiar smells and beaming so broadly he looks like a giant troll rediscovering Valhalla. "It takes a while to get back in the groove, to remember each other's ins and outs. The main thing I have to do is get him focused. It is going to take two or three shows to get back in rhythm with him, and for him to get serious again about showing." She gazes at him lovingly, admiring his sturdy, muscular frame and resolute expression. She jokes, "Maybe he and I will go on the lam together. We'll just run away and loaf on a Caribbean beach, sip margaritas, and bask in the sun." Instead, they spend two weeks in hard training: jogging and trotting uphill to tone his body, working on stand-stays to hone his attention span. Jane implores Mimi to buy her a special dog treadmill that she can use to exercise Rusty during icy winter days when she cannot risk taking him outside, where he might slip and injure himself. The dollar signs for Rusty's two handlers and jet-set life are giving Mimi headaches, and she pleads with Jane to wait on the treadmill and do the best she can.

Rusty and Jane return to the show ring in January at the Wallkill Kennel Club show in Middletown, New York. Thorn isn't there, but Rusty's old antagonist from the Greenwich Specialty is: Briart's Solar Power (Sunny), the long, tall champion handled by his owner, Barbara Heck.

Despite her work alone with him at home, Jane knows Rusty needs a refresher with spectators around, so ten minutes before the first class of Bullmastiffs are to be judged, she brings him into the ring. With several hundred people gathered around waiting for the competition, Rusty fidgets, unfocused, distracted by the noise and commotion. Jane gives a yank on his leash, causing his collar to clench around his neck for an instant, but even this correction doesn't totally command his attention. She gives him a stand-stay command, gathers the leash and gives him another yank. But this time, her hand slips as she jerks upward and her thumb flies up, poking her own eye in such a way that her fingernail cuts her just below the brow. Blood gushes. By the time Rusty is called into the ring with four males and two bitches for Best of Breed competition, Jane has a big swatch over one eye, and Rusty is still fidgeting. Wallkill, of course, is an indoor show; the heat in the building makes Rusty fret even more. Worst of all, a dense, brawny specimen like him is clearly not this judge's cup of tea. The leggy ones who move like agile Thoroughbreds get all the attention; Rusty, who pads around the ring like a rhino at a trot, is of little interest. So it is no surprise that Sunny takes the blue ribbon and Rusty comes away empty-pawed.

"I could make him a multitime best in show winner," Jane declares afterward, undaunted by the loss and delighted to be teamed with him again. "If I can get his mind centered, get him absolutely focused on showing in the ring, he could do very well at the Garden, too. I know Roy Stenmark, who will be the breed judge there; I have shown under him; but the dogs I have shown have always been giants who could fly, so I don't know how he'll respond to a tightly packed guy like Rusty. That I cannot control; but what I can do is get Rusty sharp. And I can pray. That is what I did when I won with Ned at the Garden after having only one weekend to prepare him. I prayed: 'Heavenly Father, keep this dog together.' And it happened. Ned was more together for the time we were in that ring than any show before or since. That day at the Garden, there wasn't any other dog in the world who had the power to distract your attention from him. He was a miracle, truly. I believe that most of our great wins are supernatural kinds of things. When Martin took the breed at Twin Brooks in New Jersey, it was early in the morning, so I went to church right afterward and church was the wildest it has ever been. Crazy. Inspired. When I came back to the show early in the afternoon, I guaranteed to Mimi that we would take the group. She told me that if we did, I could have anything I wanted. I said 'Two new Michelin tires for my van.' We won, and I said to Mimi, 'What do I get if we take the show?'

" 'Anything, anything at all,' Mimi told me. That was the day Martin won Best in Show, over three thousand dogs. And I got four new Michelins. God never fails, buddy. Never."

CHAPTER 12

Motherhood

At the beginning of November, Champion Allstar's Blossom
Dearie takes occupancy of a guest bedroom at Mimi Einstein's
Westchester house. Gingerly pushing open the door one afternoon, we find her sitting comfortably on her haunches atop a
twin bed, watching a talk show on which the host introduces
the day's guests as Women Who Wish Their Husbands Were
More Sexually Adventurous. Blossom rolls her large, soulful
eyes between us and the TV screen. One big canine tooth
snaggles up from her lower jaw, pushing her upper lip into a
serene sneer. The volume is turned low and the lights are dim;
Blossom is at ease, but tired.

Despite the creature comforts and the hypnotic drone of
the talk show, Blossom cannot relax because her attention is
also focused on her baby. The veteran bitch, mother of Rusty
and of many other Allstar champions, has just had her last
puppy—a litter of one, after which her uterus was surgically
removed. The single puppy, named Allstar's Sophie Tucker,
rests in a cardboard box placed inside a larger wooden whelping box under a heat lamp a few feet from Blossom's day bed.
Inside the box with the week-old baby are tube socks rolled
into ovals to help her think she is part of a full litter rather
than a singleton. Sophie is six inches long and weighs about
four pounds. She is buff brown with a tiny black mask. Her
head is round as a plum, and she has fat little paws with

smooth, unscuffed pads. Her eyes are starting to open, but despite the world seeping in, she is little more than a sensory creature who mews for food, whimpers for comfort, and growls when she is annoyed.

This one puppy is a small victory and a source of tremendous consternation for Mimi Einstein. Aside from the psychological problems a litter of one must overcome—a lone puppy doesn't naturally learn play, sharing, and other dog-to-dog social skills—one single offspring also does very little to alleviate the puppy shortage that has been an increasing dilemma at Allstar Kennel for nearly two years. The last big litter to come around was in January 1994: thirteen pups out of Allstar's Gracie Allen by Allstar's Nathan Detroit. That litter was too big. Gracie could feed only half of them at a time, which meant the other half had to be bottle fed, nearly round the clock. It was arduous, but at least Mimi was able to get an Allstar dog to thirteen of the several dozen people on her waiting list who want one. Since then, Allstar has produced just one male puppy, Sam's Sonny Boy, whom Mimi kept, and now Sophie.

It's not that Mimi didn't breed her dogs for two years; the shortage occurred because so many things went wrong. A long and productive fertile period ended without reason and a circus of catastrophes ushered in a two-year dry spell. One after another brood bitch proved infertile; some miscarried, others resorbed the puppies in their wombs. Then Mimi's topproducing stud dog developed prostate trouble and had to be neutered. ("Shall I bronze the testicles?" the veterinarian asked Mimi when she brought him in for the operation.) Mimi's phone and fax rang round the clock with people who had placed orders for puppies and wondered where they were. She began to worry that a few more years like this and Allstar Kennel would be history.

With her waiting list growing ridiculously long, Mimi took two prolific bitches, Allstar's Blossom Dearie and Allstar's Dale Evans, up to Allstar's Mugsy Malone, who is owned by Ken and Debbie Vargas and who lives with them in Stonington, Connecticut. Before bringing the bitches to him, Mimi had her vet draw blood daily to check progesterone levels, but somehow the test results proved inconclusive so she had to make a best guess as to when the time was right to inseminate them. To reduce the risks and hazards of normal procreation, the breeding was done artificially, the sperm retrieved manually from Mugsy and inserted into the vaginas of Dale and Blossom. To cover the moment of peak fertility, each female was inseminated for five days in a row.

Robust Mugsy was called on each day for his fluids, but even he proved not to be an endless font of motile sperm. Sixty-three days after the intensive artificial insemination session, the result was no puppies for Dale and the single one, Sophie Tucker, for Blossom.

It was time for desperate measures. Mimi had progressed beyond all the obvious methods of making dog babies. The old-fashioned way—throwing together a healthy male and a female in heat and letting nature take its course—is rarely used by serious breeders of show dogs. For the big or aggressive breeds in particular, it can be too risky; all that physical to-and-fro can injure a precious stud or brood bitch, and there is no guarantee of a successful consummation. As for ordinary artificial insemination, for which sperm is retrieved from the male and inserted into the female, it too is imperfect because of all the biochemical hazards and obstacles that exist for ejaculate between testis and egg. "I knew that it was time to go all the way with this thing or I would not have any more puppies," Mimi declared.

She selected as a test couple her youngest and healthiest

bitch, the new champion, Allstar's Sugar of Abby Road, and her beloved brindle stud, Sam. As Sugar neared the fertile time in her cycle, she was brought to the Framingham, Massachusetts, office of veterinarian Anita Migday, a specialist in canine fertility. There, blood was drawn from her each day and sent overnight to a laboratory in Pennsylvania that looked not only at the progesterone level, but also at the LH—luteinizing hormone. Exactly five days after the LH peaks is the optimum time for fertilization. When Mimi got the word from Pennsylvania, she threw Sam in her van and drove him to Dr. Migday's. Sperm was retrieved from Sam. Sugar was anesthetized, then cut open and her uterus incised so the fresh sperm could be deposited directly.

Twenty-five days after the surgery, Mimi goes to Veterinarian Alan Green of Katonah, New York, for a sonogram to see if Sugar is in whelp. Overhead lights are dimmed in the surgery, where a half-shaved hound in a wire-fronted cage moans in pain, just stitched up after an encounter with a raccoon. Sugar lies on the floor, surrounded by Mimi, two vet techs, and Dr. Green, who bears a cheerful resemblance to comedian Albert Brooks. The two-year-old bitch proves to be remarkably amiable as cold conducting gel is squirted on her stomach and the probe slides around. "There's one," Dr. Green announces after a while when he spots a shifting shape on the monitor that he recognizes as a puppy in the making. "There's another," he says after several long moments searching the womb.

Mimi sighs with some relief, but then, like a craps shooter on a roll, she orders, "Keep counting."

"There's another," the vet says tentatively. "They are very small now, but don't worry that anything is wrong . . . and another . . . and that's five. . . . That's the left side, so far." He then adjust the machine, trying to see better. "She is a gassy girl," he says, referring to the blur out of which the embryonic puppies are appearing. "This is like flying through a fog. I've got five so far . . . six . . . seven." At that, he stops counting. Mimi relaxes.

The assistants and vet congratulate her, but the moment of triumph quickly passes. Never content to rest on her victories, Mimi now has new and other things to worry about. Sugar's mother has a history of spontaneous abortions. Could that mean she should be on hormone therapy to prevent it from happening to her? Also, the vet wants to draw blood to check for herpes—another potential threat to the litter's survival.

Before leaving the office, Mimi grabs a moment of Dr. Green's time for yet another concern. The two of them have a special relationship that goes beyond her high regard for him as a practitioner. Theirs is a mutual respect and close friendship developed over years of all the crises, emergencies, and joys that go with breeding dogs. "As I left the house, Edie vomited," she tells him, referring to a brood bitch in her kennel. "I'm wondering if I should start her on antibiotics for Lyme disease."

"Maybe she vomited for no good reason," Green submits, knowing Mimi's tendency to worry.

"What bothers me is that she didn't eat the vomit," Mimi counters.

Dr. Green suppresses a smile. "Maybe this vomit didn't taste as good as the usual vomit," he suggests.

"Right," Mimi says skeptically as she steers Sugar out to the parking lot and the waiting van, adding under her breath: "A lot he knows. . . ."

On December 14, Sugar delivers three babies in a cesarean operation performed in Alan Green's office: one brindle bitch that Mimi decides to keep, and a red bitch and red male destined for the homes of two patient people on the waiting list.

Apparently four embryonic puppies were absorbed in the womb.

Sugar is not a good mother. She has so little milk a bottle must be used to supplement her teats; and she has no enthusiasm for cleaning and mothering the pups. As Sugar sleeps, oblivious to her responsibilities, Mimi cancels her annual New Year's Eve party and instead spends the night bottle-feeding puppies, who need to suckle every four hours. After their midnight meal, Mimi manages to stretch the schedule to get six hours' sleep before having to prepare their formula again before dawn.

Just after the age of two weeks, the red female baby develops tremors. Whenever she tries to move, her entire body shakes uncontrollably. She is otherwise healthy—eager to eat, growing normally, tail-wagging happy when she frolics with her litter mates. But the palsy is so extreme that she cannot eat unless Mimi holds her tight to steady her as she pushes her little face into the dish of warm formula. It is heartbreaking to watch the tiny creature gripped by a powerful unknown affliction, and Mimi is frantic. Having never seen this condition, she calls Dr. Migday in Massachusetts, who faxes down a chapter from a veterinary text titled "Ataxia, Paresis, and Paralysis." The dense technical prose suggests several diagnoses with such forbidding names as truncal ataxia, canine cerebellar hypoplasia, and hypomyeliniation dysmyliniation. The prognosis for the latter, if that's what's wrong with the puppy, is good: spontaneous improvement by eight to twelve months, with no apparent residual effects. After examining the puppy and consulting with colleagues at Cornell School of Veterinary Medicine, Dr. Green's opinion is optimistic: The puppy has a good chance of growing out of her condition.

In over a dozen years breeding Bullmastiffs, Mimi has never had a puppy with the shakes; and although veterinarians don't know if it is hereditary, no scrupulous breeder would allow the possibility of such an affliction being passed on. Therefore, the puppy must be spayed; her otherwise good All-star genes are lost to posterity.

While the puppy's anguish is a rarity, genetic deficiency is an issue all breeders of purebred dogs must deal with. Because they rely on selective breeding, they all inbreed to a certain degree in hopes of maintaining and magnifying the best qualities of their best dogs. The result is that not only beauty, but also flaws, are perpetuated and amplified. In a muckraking cover story about what it called a "national canine health crisis" in December 1994, *Time* magazine revealed that one in four purebred dogs is afflicted with some serious genetic malady. Hip dysplasia is rampant among German Shepherds and Golden Retrievers; deafness plagues Dalmations; giant breeds such as Great Danes and Newfoundlands are prone to heart attacks. Bullmastiffs have been relatively fortunate because they are a breed that has not been tremendously exaggerated (like Bulldogs with their flat faces and consequent breathing problems or needle-nosed Collies with their small brain pans); nor have they ever been a big fad that has encouraged willy-nilly production by unscrupulous breeders who only wanted to make a profit (as has happened in the past to Saint Bernards and Cocker Spaniels). But even if it mostly has been tended by responsible breeders who value health over beauty, the Bullmastiff's very limited gene pool swirls with weaknesses and hazards: cruciate ligaments that tend to tear, arthritic hips, thyroid deficiency, dermatological disorders. And now, maybe, something new: uncontrollable tremors.

"What am I going to do with a dog who's got the shakes?" Mimi laments one cold January afternoon as she holds the trembling puppy's face to a dish with softened kibble in the formula—her first exposure to solid food. "This is supposed to be the one that goes to that southern lawyer. He wanted a bitch, specifically one of Sugar's, so this one should be his. His family even has her name picked out—Allstar Katonah's Pocahontas. But how can I show her to him like this? I don't even know if she'll ever get better. What if it takes eight months? What if I have to put her down? It is a whole lot easier if there is something wrong right from the beginning, and you know it, and you never bring the puppy home. But by now, I know her and I like her. She is growing fine. She is the biggest of the three and the best eater and she always wants to play with the others. It is hideous to see her shake so bad she cannot move."

Mimi grips the helpless three-week-old tight enough in one hand so she doesn't shake as she eagerly laps up her 2:30 P.M. meal. Her black mask drips milk as she joyously licks her lips, and her soft pink belly inflates with food like a little balloon. One long, satisfied burp signals she is done, and Mimi sets her back down under the heat lamp in the whelping box, where she is seized once again by convulsions. With characteristic understatement and no tears in her eyes, Mimi says quietly, "I tell you, it is going to be very unpleasant if I have to put this girl down."

The time has come to make a decision about Sugar, the puppies' mother. Theoretically, she is showable—she did fabulously well early in the season—but Mimi doesn't especially want to campaign her because she doesn't have the big head and massive physique that are Allstar's hallmarks. Even if she can win, there would be no point in campaigning a dog whose looks don't represent the standard as Mimi firmly believes it ought to be represented. Furthermore, it turns out that young Sugar, who was Mimi's pampered baby in the spring, doesn't get along at all with the venerable Doris Day, Mimi's beloved old brood bitch (long since spayed), who enjoys the privilege of run-of-the-house along with Sam. The two bitches now have to be separated, which means Sugar is relegated to a run in the kennel. "She is a fabulous dog who shouldn't be living out there," Mimi says. "She should be living happily in someone's home."

At the age of five weeks, the shaking puppy stops shaking. It happens in an instant. The tremors stop and her movements are completely normal. She joins her two littermates galloping across the floors of the house, slipping and tumbling and crashing into furniture as happy puppies like to do, showing no residual symptoms whatsoever. In fact, she becomes the dominant of the three, regularly giving hell to her siblings and making sure she always gets the most food. Mimi can now find a home for her . . . but it must be a home where she will not be bred. Whatever strange neurological demons tormented her might possibly be hereditary; if so, it is a breeder's duty to stop their spread.

A week after the puppy's spontaneous recovery, Mimi takes the threesome to veterinarian Alan Green for shots to begin building their immunities against distemper, flu, and parvovirus. In a routine exam, Dr. Green discovers that the red male has a heart murmur. The doctor doesn't have equipment sophisticated enough to determine precisely how serious it is: It might be nothing to worry about, or it could require a cardiologist to operate so the young pup can live beyond his first birthday. In either case, diagnosis requires a grueling trip to the Animal Medical Center in New York City where Mimi and the tiny patient spend hours in a waiting room reminiscent of Bellevue hospital on Saturday night but with the added tumult of yelping dogs, crying cats, and screeching birds. When the veterinarian finally examines the puppy, who by now has missed his feeding and is shivering from stress, the sonogram proves inconclusive and the doctor tells Mimi she should bring the dog back for another exam. Mimi is furious. She is outraged by the chaos of the hospital and the futility of the exam. She is so worried for the weakened puppy that she storms out without stopping at the cashier to pay the several-hundred-dollar bill. "I don't know if I ought to pay them," she fumes. "I doubt if they can find me anyway. They had me down in their records as Mimi Feinstein." The bill does finally get to her, and she does send them a check . . . along with an angry letter to the hospital board.

Mimi brings the puppy back to Dr. Green, where they decide to call in a surgeon specializing in soft tissue operations. If the defect can be repaired handily, it will be done. If it proves to be more complicated or fundamentally incurable, the puppy will be put to sleep then and there. Fortunately, the condition is readily fixed in surgery—the pulmonary artery and aorta, connected by a vessel that is supposed to close at birth but never did, are separated properly. However, when the puppy revives, he has terrible trouble breathing. Dr. Green tells Mimi that the respiratory distress is due to one of two things. It might be caused by swelling of the trachea from the trauma caused by intubation of the anesthetic; or it is possible a nerve was affected in surgery, partially paralyzing the esophagus. He treats the puppy with cortisone and sends it home with Mimi.

"This is the worst thing I have ever seen," Mimi laments late the afternoon of the operation when she calls friends to tell them the operation was a success, but the patient seems to be dying. "He is lying on his bed, staring up at me with his big eyes, pleading for help. He is heaving, whistling, strangling; he is in terrible distress, and I can do nothing to help him."

She takes the suffering animal back to Dr. Green, who performs an emergency tracheotomy, using a makeshift tube that is later replaced with a proper one retrieved from a nearby children's hospital. The young dog can now breathe easily, but the tube must be suctioned every three hours, which would require hiring a round-the-clock technician. However, Dr. Green, who has become very attached to the needy puppy, assumes this responsibility himself, taking the puppy home and keeping it by his bed at night, nestled in a laundry basket.

This sickly puppy's problems are complicated by the fact that he has already been spoken for. A nice couple has been to Mimi's house twice to see him. "They are in love with him already," Mimi grieves, and they are willing to take him despite all that has happened. Of course, the dog cannot be bred; and the money Mimi has spent (an estimated four thousand dollars) is three times what the new owners will pay for him, if he survives, and if the couple still wants him, surgery and all.

Two days after the puppy's heart condition is discovered, the elderly Doris Day stops eating. Doris is Mimi's oldest and most cherished dog, the one out of all she has known who means the most to her, her constant companion around the house. Doris has remained relatively healthy to the ripe old (for a Bullmastiff) age of ten-and-a-half. Long since spayed, she is the mother, grandmother, or great-grandmother of nearly every good dog Allstar Kennel has produced. For years after her show ring career, Doris worked with Mimi as a therapy dog in the nursing home project Mimi founded, called Golden Outreach. Together, the two of them visited elderly patients who had no families left, or whose families had abandoned them, and as they did so, a deep bond developed between Mimi and the kindly old dog with whom she shared so much emotional hurt. Some of the forgotten souls with whom they spent time had withdrawn almost completely from any connection with others; but as sometimes happens, the steadfast presence of a calm and benevolent animal by their side helped them escape their solitude. Mimi recalls one such woman who, when she reached the end, pleaded for Doris to come be with her as she died.

Now slow and gaunt herself, Doris Day commands the run of the house with Sam; and whatever she requires to be happy, Mimi is only too happy to provide. A few months earlier, when Doris developed a tumor on her foot and had to have a toe amputated, Mimi debated the wisdom of anesthetizing and operating on such an old creature. But Doris was so precious, the risk seemed worthwhile. With some hyperbole perhaps, Mimi told the doctors she would pay a million dollars to keep Doris well. But money cannot save her now. She has terminal cancer. Even Mimi's hope that cortisone injections might buy Doris a week or two of comfort before the end proves futile. The cancer has metastasized and no drug can alleviate her pain.

Doris doesn't like the veterinarian's office, so Mimi will not have her put to sleep there. But she does like rides in the car. So Mimi loads her into the Astrovan, as Doris was loaded into vans on dog show weekends many years ago when she was a young competitor. This time, though, there is no glory or blue ribbon at the end of the road. As she sits in the car in the parking lot of the vet's office, her old Bullmastiff brow furrows with worry. A tourniquet is bound around her right front leg and the doctor slides a needle with a powerful sedative into a vein. Doris falls asleep, then dies.

The decision to put her down in the car is also a practical one. The procedure finished, the unwieldy corpse can stay in the vehicle and be transported directly to Mimi's SPCA shelter to be cremated.

"I am thinking of getting out of this business altogether," Mimi proclaims with profound sadness after it is all over. "Purebred dogs are nothing but heartache. I just want nice mutts from the pound who live forever."

CHAPTER 13

The Dark Horse

The death of Doris, the frustrations of impotence and infertility, then the physically exhausting and heartbreaking work of caring for sick puppies have worn Mimi Einstein to a frazzle by January. "I need to get away from all this," she repeats like a litany as the heavy winter snows make her feel all the more a prisoner of a house full of demanding Bullmastiffs. "I have to see the sun. I have to go someplace where there are no puppies desperately needing me." The stresses of breeding are exasperating; but what also gnaw at Mimi are the year's disappointments in the show ring. It has not been a triumphant time for Allstar Kennel; for the first time in many years, Allstar dogs are not a major presence in the winner's circle.

Although she feels fed up and exhausted from all that has transpired, Mimi does not turn away from the show ring. On the contrary. Her desperation makes her all the more excited about the Westminster Kennel Club show coming up at Madison Square Garden in mid-February. Here is one grand opportunity to right all the year's wrongs, to reverse a streak of bad fortune, and to end the season with a decisive success. She has done it before, just two years earlier, when Allstar's Nathan Detroit came out of nowhere to take the breed and make Allstar the kennel to beat. A victory like that would be a jackpot so sweet that it would wipe out all the pain of a long season of disappointments. Now, like a back-against-the-wall card sharp

147

at a stud poker table, Mimi begins to feel the thrill of playing the long shot when the chips are down.

Itchy as she is for the competition, she knows she does not hold a terrific hand. Sam never even earned his championship. Nathan Detroit, whom she hoped to resurrect as Allstar's savior, is lame and out of contention. Sonny Boy is still too young. Rusty is back and Jane is whipping him into shape, but he has no momentum whatsoever coming into the Westminster show. If she is to have any hope of doing well at the Garden, Mimi needs an ace in the hole. She shuffles and reshuffles the deck, looking for an answer.

And she draws Mugsy Malone. Mugsy, a five-year-old dark red male, is one of the best dogs to come out of Mimi's kennel: the top-winning Bullmastiff of 1993 and a quintessential example of what she thinks the breed should look like. He is huge, luxuriously muscled, straight and square from every angle, and he has a head to stop traffic. His last appearance in the show ring was the summer of 1994 at the New England Bullmastiff Association specialty show in Providence, where he won the Best of Breed, then moved up and won over the entire Working Group, and very nearly took another Best in Show. Few Bullmastiffs ever rise above all the other breeds to win Best in Show. Mugsy did it three times at the peak of his career, when he seemed unstoppable.

Although he is an Allstar dog, out of Allstar's Hawk's Flight Koa by Allstar's Terry Thomas, Mimi doesn't own Mugsy Malone. Mugsy lives in Stonington, Connecticut, with Ken and Debbie Vargas, who bought him as a puppy in 1990. The Vargases, who had never owned a Bullmastiff before, thought it might be fun to show him some day, but basically he was raised as a pet. Growing up, Mugsy was treated as one of the guys. At Ken's rowdy keg parties, he lapped beer out of the spill bucket; and when Ken and his pals went camping,

Ken used Mugsy as a pillow, resting his head on the dog's beefy barrel chest.

When he was seven months old, the Vargases drove down to Westchester County, New York, so Mimi could have a look at him and tell them if she thought it would be worth taking him into the ring. When Mimi saw Mugsy step out of the car, her adrenaline began to pump. He was a thrill to see. Many of the large breed dogs, when they grow as fast and as big as Mugsy, look awkward—*too* big, lumbering, uncomfortable—but Mugsy had become a giant athlete who moved with the spring of a terrier and the force of a rolling boulder. His coat was a gorgeous burnished red; his mask was dark and his amber eyes sparkled with an expression of utmost resolve. Mimi recalls, "I looked at him, and I said to myself, *here is a once-in-a-lifetime dog, a dog who has it all.*"

In the fall of 1991, Mugsy Malone finished his championship by winning three-point majors on each of three consecutive days. At his full fighting weight of one hundred sixty pounds, he did not merely look like a good example of the breed; he had charisma. Judges and spectators alike could see that this was a dog who savored his moment in the show ring and basked in people's admiration. For Mugsy, the applause of the crowd was like a victory cheer, infusing his trot with jubilation that could only be described as a dog's dance of joy.

After Mugsy won his championship, Mimi, who had become the neophyte Vargases' mentor in the show ring, asked them, "What are you going to do now? Are you going to continue?"

" 'Continue'? We didn't understand," Debbie remembers. She and Ken had assumed that a championship would be the climax of Mugsy's show career—as high as you go. But when Mimi explained that his championship was just the beginning and that they could now show him as a special in Best of

Breed classes, win the breed, then go on to win over all the other breeds in the Working Group, and possibly go even higher, to Best in Show, it didn't take much convincing. The Vargases had tasted sweet victory; and Mugsy was so good, and enjoyed it so much, they felt they owed him unconditional support. Under Mimi's guidance, they began placing advertisements boasting of his wins in the major dog show publications and they retained professional handler Fred Olsen to take him into the ring. The Vargases, new to the show circuit, estimate they spent $25,000 campaigning Mugsy—a relatively small amount of money for a top show dog, reflecting the fact that he never traveled to compete outside the Northeast. But despite their limited investment, Mugsy swiftly became the top-winning Bullmastiff in the nation, showering them—as well as Allstar Kennel—with glory. It was a stunning accomplishment, for Working Group competition is the most ferocious in the Northeast. It would have been so much easier for him to win the group in other parts of the country. But by the time he was three years old, Mugsy Malone was a dog who could, and did, beat any other dog of any other breed, anytime, anywhere.

In November 1993, Mugsy's leg blew out. He jumped out the back of the Vargases' parked Blazer, as he always did at shows, and when he went around the ring that day, he looked like Mickey Mantle circling the bases on an off-day—injured and in pain, yet still a glory of the sport. He had an operation to repair a torn ligament and in 1994, after eight months' absence, he reappeared in the show ring at the specialty in Providence, where he took Best of Breed and Best in Group. Then, he went lame again, at which point the Vargases retired him from competition so he could spend his time siring puppies.

But there was one big prize Mugsy never won during his short, stellar career: Best of Breed at Westminster. Now, encouraged by Mimi, they decide to enter him in the West-minster Kennel Club show, but to tell only their closest friends. This, they figure, will give Mugsy a psychological edge. For a handler blithely campaigning some other Bullmastiff around the country and expecting to do well at the Garden, the sight of Mugsy Malone back in the ring at the big show is going to be like a jockey on a good horse sizing up his competition down the starting gate and suddenly spotting Secretariat among his rivals.

"He deserves the Garden," Ken says. "He is too good a dog not to win there." The Vargases' ambitions for Mugsy are abetted by Mimi, who knows that if he is fit and if he can radiate his patented allure, no dog can beat him. He could be All-star's best shot at a victory in Madison Square Garden.

Rather than warm him up in lesser venues to prepare for the summit of the dog show world, the Vargases believe their best strategy is to protect his weak leg. "One hundred percent containment," Debbie says, joking. "If I could put him in a full body cast, I would."

For many dogs, a life of rest and relaxation would be a boon. But Mugsy likes to play like he always did when he was young. In the large, fenced yard of the Vargases' spacious country home, he chases after birds and squirrels like a puppy. In his room, which he shares with two of his progeny, Milo and Molly, he has an immense wire crate that he stays in; but when people walk in the door to visit him, he stands up and the crate suddenly looks very small, more like a garment of chain mail than a containment device. When he moves, his crate moves, too; and when finally the door is opened and he is free, he is so overjoyed with company that he effortlessly rears up and puts his front paws on your shoulders, engulfing you with gusts of hot breath in a face-to-face canine embrace.

At Christmas 1995, less than two months away from the

Westminster show, he appears absolutely sound, as vigorous as a youngster, eager to win again. But in January, when Mimi Einstein comes to visit, she sniffs trouble. Although Mugsy does not belong to her, Mimi dotes on him like one of her own. In the most meaningful sense among dog breeders, he *is* hers. "Along with Martin, he is the best dog Allstar has ever produced," she proclaims.

"Oh, my God!" she cries when she walks into the Vargases' modern ranch house, looks out the glass doors that lead to their fenced-in backyard, and spots Mugsy Malone cheerfully loping across the grass, trailing long ropes of drool that stiffen in the icy winter winds. "What is he doing outside?" Mimi cries to the heavens.

"I thought you were watching him," Ken says to Debbie. Under Mimi's tough headmistressing, the Vargases—two strong, mature, assertive adults—quickly become scared kids.

"I wouldn't have had to let him out alone if *someone* had bothered to walk him earlier," Debbie says in her own defense.

It is an embarrassing moment. The Vargases have been caught by their guru doing the unthinkable with a prize dog: letting him run free on treacherously icy ground just weeks before Westminster.

"One bad step and February twelfth goes down the drain," Mimi cautions, fully aware of Mugsy's history of leg injuries. "He shouldn't even be here. He should be in a small run at Fred Olsen's," she says.

A long moment passes. No one speaks as Mimi scrutinizes the dog frolicking through the yard.

"He looks good," she allows cautiously as the big red champion bounds in the door, thrilled to see her. Although she is seldom openly emotional about the dogs she loves, Mimi virtually laughs with pleasure as she meticulously runs her eyes over his huge head and along his muscled physique and watches how level his back remains when he runs from person to person in the Vargases' living room, sniffing everybody and depositing globules of slushy saliva on shoes and pant legs. She is looking at him the way a judge would look at him, and she cannot help but beam with joy. She strokes his head like a sculptor caressing a favorite piece of work. Suddenly she stops. The blood drains from her face. "What is this?!" she exclaims, grabbing something under the skin at the back of his neck.

"A cyst," Ken says somewhat sheepishly.

Mimi knows full well what it is. "You didn't have it taken out?"

"It's too late," Ken says. "We are hoping it will disappear."

"And what is this thing?" Mimi says, her hysteria mounting as her educated fingers move around his neck the way a judge's might move in the show ring and she finds a small place where the hair has been shaved and a scar mars the skin.

"Another cyst," Debbie admits. "We had that one removed."

"Oh, God," Mimi moans, worried that the veteran dog's minor imperfections will knock him out of competition.

"If we are meant to win, we will win," Ken announces philosophically, hitching up his athletic sweatpants and walking away from the two women. "I am not going to coop him up and worry about every little bump on his skin." He goes to the refrigerator to fetch bottles of his home brew, which he calls Mugsy Malone's Dog House Bitter. Each bottle has a gold label with a picture of Mugsy's formidable head. He pours the delicious dark amber beer into chilled mugs for company as Mugsy watches and flaps his big, pink tongue around his lips, hoping to get a draught for himself, just like the good old days when he was just one of the guys and not a show dog.

CHAPTER 14

The Beauty of the Beast

To help dogs look and feel their best, humans groom them. Grooming is natural: wild dogs and wolves do it all the time; but the methods they use are basically limited to licking one another. By comparison, domesticated canines get the royal treatment. Bathed with sweet-smelling shampoo, brushed and teased, de-matted and fluff-dried, cut and trimmed from topknot to toenails, a well-groomed dog is more than just a tour de force of cleanliness; it is a flight of fancy. In full show clip, some breeds are scarcely recognizable as animals, appearing more like undulating bathmats, flying carpets, or topiary shrubs. A plucked and stripped terrier, a properly brushed Shih Tzu, or a Standard Poodle in a continental clip with powdered pompoms will turn heads on any sidewalk as well as in the show ring.

The judging standards of most breeds forbid such affectations as colorizing a coat or painting toenails in shades of pink, and so the more elaborate cosmetology rituals are indulged more by pampered pets than by working show dogs. Nevertheless, good grooming is vital to the success of any dog that steps into the ring. Some need more than others, and there are certain breeds whose show coiffure is nothing short of spectacular—Poodles, Bichons, and Komondors, for example. But for even the shortest-coated, most minimally made-up ones, there exist tonsorial tricks and techniques that can vastly improve their appearance, and hence their chance to win blue ribbons.

The man who wrote the book on this subject—*The All-Breed Dog Grooming Guide*—is Sam Kohl, director of the New York School of Dog Grooming, to which students come from all over the world to study the art of making dogs look fabulous.

Mr. Kohl is a burly man with a full head of white, springy hair and a neatly trimmed mustache who says he has been "in dogs" since 1949. As he escorts visitors into the large grooming parlor on the second floor of his four-story academy on East Thirty-Fourth Street in Manhattan, he majestically recalls Thomas Edison: "Edison had his Menlo Park," he says, sweeping his hands across a vista of grooming tables on which four-legged clients are being worked on with shears and shedders by teams of beauticians in brown nylon barbers' jackets. "This is my Menlo Bark." Kohl is a sly character who cannot resist plays on words. "You remember the robber barons?" he asks as he shows a rubber curry comb he markets to professional pet groomers. "My brand name for these is the Rubber Barons." He also has designed bumper stickers that say CAT HOUSE OPERATOR and GROOMERS DO IT DOGGIE STYLE.

Kohl's canine conservatory, the oldest and largest such institution in the world, is also a busy salon, to which New Yorkers bring animals in need of beautification: mostly dogs, some cats, and the occasional rabbit or ferret. Starting at 7:30 in the morning, they arrive for their day of adornment and are escorted by a member of the staff to an individual waiting-room holding pen on which a small card lists their name, their preferred grooming routine, and any special instructions. The card of Chadwick, a clever-looking Cocker, notes that he will drool if a blowdryer is aimed at his snout; the card of a Papillon warns that her toes are especially sensitive. A scandalously unkempt Lhasa Apso, having rolled in God-knows-what weeks ago, waits in his crate for requisite hours of brushing and combing. Nearby, an impeccable Yorkshire Terrier, who looks stunning even though she just rolled out of bed, stands by for the usual—her once-weekly Schnauzer-type clip job that puts an exclamation point on her bold, self-confident personality.

Dogs with long fur need to be groomed regularly whether or not they are shown, but every breed can benefit from some serious barbering—a bath, a pedicure, perhaps a quick trim of the stray hairs in its ears and between its footpads. Mr. Kohl sees them all; and his salon is equipped with hydraulic tables to elevate the large breeds to eye level and with nearly microscopic combs for teacup-size Chihuahuas. One reason aspiring groomers covet enrollment in his school is its location in New York City, where, sooner or later, every breed of dog will walk through the door, thus exposing students to the widest array of grooming challenges as they apprentice here with the masters. Furthermore, Kohl points out that New York is the world's style capital, a place where dogs as well as human beings are most likely to find appreciative eyes for their chic appearance.

Some breeds go to the beauty parlor more than others. Toys, little terriers, and non-working spaniels are frequent denizens of the salons; and of course, there are always Poodles. The first day of class in every NYSDG program of study, freshmen observe an instructor do a complete Poodle job. Poodles are a breed on which an experienced groomer can show real razzle-dazzle, and therefore a good way to get students fired up about what they will be able to do when they complete the course.

Into the classroom walks an unkempt, unclipped ragamuffin, and a few hours later, out goes a buff hunk in a Royal

Dutch Clip with a high-teased topknot. "They have stars in their eyes," Sam Kohl boasts of the pupils who watch this demonstration.

Of all the types of dogs that come in, terriers are the toughest. "They're so lively," Kohl explains with great affection. "They are a handful. They want to play, or to bite. They are devils. And Wire-Haired Terriers are the worst . . . which is to say, the best. But what trouble to clip! If you really want to groom them right, you have to hand-strip them, remove all the dead hairs one by one. That is the only way to get the coat to really feel wiry, the way it's supposed to feel. I can make a pet Wire-Haired Terrier look right with just a brush, comb, and scissors in less than an hour. But it won't have the hard-wire texture you get by hand-stripping, which is what a judge looks for in the show ring."

Grooming for show can be very different from grooming for the simple purpose of making a dog look sharp. An expert groomer aiming for a blue ribbon can use shears, comb, spray, and powder to virtually reshape a contestant to better fit the standard in the same way some balding men comb their few remaining hairs over the top of their bare noggins to look more youthful. Of course, good judges are no more fooled by such tricks than most of us are by men's combovers; but when you are looking for every edge, it doesn't hurt to know how to brush the rump hair forward to emphasize the hocks' angulation or to trim around the withers in a way that shortens a too-long back.

To point out how different show grooming can be from pet grooming, Kohl recalls the time during the Westminster Kennel Club show when a Bedlington Terrier handler called him and volunteered to demonstrate a Bedlington clip to his students. He welcomed the opportunity, for Bedlingtons are fairly rare and they require elaborate scissoring techniques to achieve their highly unusual lamblike shape: cutting with the flow of the hair at the base of the tail and against it at the tip, going against the grain on the cheeks and zig-zagging on the ears, and using shears to precisely shape the head fur in such a way that the sides are flat and the topknot is full and rounded. "She did a beautiful job," he says. "But it took four hours. Later, I told my students that you cannot earn a living if it takes you four hours to trim a single dog. That is a luxury of the show ring."

The basic grooming routine for every dog at the New York School of Dog Grooming begins with toenails. Students are advised to always start at the rear so if it's an aggressive dog, you'll know it before he's in a position to attack you. All dogs are put on grooming tables with restraining loops around their necks, and in the rare case of a biter, a muzzle on its snout. After the toes are clipped, the ears are cleaned. Then the dog is brushed, then bathed and lightly toweled. After that, depending on its coat, it is either cage-dried or fluff-dried with a hand-held drier. Then come the extras, if required: shaping with shears and clippers, teasing, nail coloring, or coat tinting. "We don't like to use perfume," Kohl says. "Our shampoo smells good enough. But we do spray them with a nice cologne before they leave. We prefer Lambert K, which is fresh and clean; we do have some customers who request Ring number five, which is perfumy, like Chanel number five."

To show that dog grooming is a true craft, Kohl asks if we know how to hold a pair of scissors. We thought we did, but we were wrong. "I can see an amateur groomer in his scissors-hold," he says, demonstrating how to control them by cradling the handle of one blade in your fingers and using it to glide a pathway through the hair, while gently using only the tip of your thumb to work the other blade up and down, thus cutting like a guillotine rather than chopping like pruning shears. Such techniques, as well as the individual peculiarities of some 150 different breeds, are taught to students over a course of 300 hours, ranging from ten weeks—if you attend Monday through Friday, all day—to fifty weeks of Saturdays only. Tuition for the full course is $3,600, plus $323.67 worth of equipment, plus a $200 dormitory fee for five weeks if you need a place to stay. Dorm rooms are on the two floors above the school, many of them occupied by foreign students.

"I love the ones from Japan," Kohl says. "Dogs are big there, and the students are so enthusiastic. To be a successful groomer, you need that enthusiasm, for people as well as for their pets. We don't want our groomers to be amateurish—no cooing and hugging of the dogs—they have to be professional; but they also need to love what they do. A great groomer needs not only passion; he must also have empathy and patience and a nice low-key temperament. You need to know how to make everybody relax—the dogs and the people who bring them in.

"A groomer sees all kinds of people," Mr. Kohl says, launching into one of his favorite stories, about the "Two tough ladies, garment-center ladies . . . half-models, if you know what I mean . . . a couple of tomatoes. The first one had loaned the other one $3,700, and the other one didn't want to pay it back. So the one who wanted her money sent in a friend to pick up the other one's dog, who was here for grooming. We released the dog, and later that day the other one came in and started screaming, 'Where's my dog? Barbara stole my dog!' She called in her lawyer and we got sued for five million, one thousand dollars. The million was for pain and suffering; the thousand was for lost-dog flyers she printed up. I thought I was going to lose everything, but then the police found her dog wandering in the streets. They put it in a patrol car and brought it to the SPCA. The lady claimed it wasn't really hers, but she took it anyway and dropped the suit."

As for the old chestnut that animals resemble their owners, Mr. Kohl tends to agree, but with some reservations. "You know Dr. Atkins, the diet doctor?" he says. "He had six Old English Sheepdogs he used to bring in. Every one of them was overweight." Of course, obesity in a long-haired dog is but a small challenge to an accomplished dog groomer, who can ingeniously disguise the extra pounds with a tight clip on the underchest, flanks, and rump.

A professional groomer needs to be ready to handle everything, from hand-separating the Rastafarian cords of a Komondor's coat to tapering the featherings of an Irish Setter's tail. Like any fashion trade, dog grooming is fickle. Not only do fur styles change, breeds themselves come in and out of vogue. "For many years, all we saw were Old English Sheepdogs," Mr. Kohl recalls. "They are hard to groom because they require so much scissoring and frequent de-matting. There was a time back in the late 1970s that we cursed them, there were so many coming in. They were the bread and butter of our business, but now sometimes I wonder, did people eat them all? We see so few of them. After them, it was Lhasas and Shih Tzus, which are similar in their grooming requirements, but smaller, so they don't get as badly matted. There was a Cocker Spaniel spurt for a while, then people started buying Akitas, and now Rottweilers. Today, everybody wants a low-maintenance dog. It's the economy."

Fewer people these days request their dog's nails be colored with polish, as was popular in the 1960s, although bright red toenails are more popular in New York than anyplace else, Mr. Kohl reveals. Dye jobs, for which a dog's coat is tinted an unnatural pink or aqua to match its leash or its master's home decor, were once a staple of the grooming business—the vestibule of the school has an advertisement on the wall with a lady walking a powder-blue Poodle—but such rococo rituals have become quite rare, too. One thing people are requesting more and more these days, but the New York School of Dog Grooming will not do, is to pierce a dog's ears so it can wear earrings. "That is a veterinarian's job," Mr. Kohl declares.

CHAPTER 15

Madison Square Garden

The Westminster Kennel Club all-breed show is not just another dog show. It is the event of the year. For tens of millions of people who own purebred dogs in this country, it is the Kentucky Derby of canines, where the best of the best are ordained. For those who breed dogs, winning it is the great gold ring, the top of the world.

Held every year since 1877, Westminster is the oldest dog show in the country, the second-oldest American sporting contest of any kind, after the Derby; and it is older by nine years than England's famous Crufts dog show—the world's largest. Staged in Madison Square Garden each year on a Monday and Tuesday in February, it attracts 2,500 of the nation's top dogs as well as thousands of fanciers and hundreds of journalists from newspapers and television stations that don't ordinarily carry dog show news. All around New York, dog people celebrate with parties, banquets, and awards presentations. The weekend before the event, some thirty different breed clubs hold specialty matches in the area; Saturday night before the show, Ken-L Ration sponsors a black-tie banquet to which the year's top dogs are invited with their owners and handlers.

Dog shows have changed a lot since Westminster began with 1,100 entries at Gillmore's Garden in New York in 1877. In the early days, the very idea of a purebred dog was something of a novelty. Even the concept of a genteel dog show was strange, considering that the popular canine entertainments through much of the nineteenth century had been bull-baiting, in which ferocious fighting dogs brought down bovines, and ratting, in which terriers killed as many rats as they could in the shortest possible time. As humane societies fought against such bloody activities, and legislatures in England and America outlawed them, a newer, kinder way to appreciate dogs was developed. The first dog show was staged in 1859 in Newcastle-on-Tyne in northern England, where pointers and setters used for hunting were brought into the ring so judges could compare their nose, pace, and range. Fourteen years later, the Kennel Club of Great Britain was established, and the next year, 1874, shows were first held in America, in Chicago and New York State.

At the earliest American dog shows, animals were exhibited in an atmosphere that was as much carnival bazaar as it was formal sport. Most of the familiar modern breeds had not yet been developed, and pedigrees were rare among the animals that were shown. Classes at the first Westminster contests included "red setters exhibited by ladies" and "English setters, either sex." Canine curiosities were often part of the show. A wild Australian dingo was brought to the 1880 exhibition, its address listed as "Central Park Menagerie." That same year, a Saint Bernard-Siberian Bloodhound cross named Nero was advertised as having been the very dog who had been put "in charge of the first baby elephant that was ever exhibited in America." The 1877 show featured a single "Esquimaux Dog," a "Lion Dog," a Siberian Bloodhound, an exceptional pooch named Nellie who walked on her back legs because the front ones were missing, and Queen Victoria's own Scottish Deerhounds, named Oscar and Dagmar, who were available for purchase at $50,000 apiece. In 1889 a

Siberian Wolfhound with an unknown pedigree was listed with a price tag of $10,000; his breeder: the Czar of Russia. With the exception of a Maltese Terrier described in the 1890 catalogue as "priceless," it was common in those days to put a price on all dogs brought into competition—a pecuniary practice long since abandoned. And in contrast to today's simple ribbons and trophies, the top dog at the first Westminster show won for his master a precious gold-engraved pearl-handled revolver.

Dogs of real use to hunters were then the focus of the show ring, which existed primarily as an adjunct to the shooting sports. The Westminster Kennel Club's logo is still a dog on point—the legendary Sensation, imported by the WKC from England. Over the years, however, field dogs were joined by other, less outdoorsy breeds as stud books for them were created; and the Westminster entry has become a very good reflection of prevailing dog fashions. Saint Bernards crowded the ring at the turn of the century when America became infatuated with them; big entries of Scotties were fielded in the 1930s, no doubt inspired by FDR's White House pet, Fala; and in the decade after My Own Brucie, a Cocker Spaniel, won two consecutive Best in Show ribbons at Westminster in 1940 and 1941, the Garden was flooded with Cockers. For 1996, the contest features more Shar-Peis than either Labradors or Golden Retrievers—a whopping forty-six of the now-popular wrinkled canine that *Life* magazine declared "the world's rarest dog" just ten years before!

It is a blistering cold ten degrees in New York on Monday, February 12, when the show begins inside Madison Square Garden at 8:30 in the morning. Exhibitors and their entourages as well as experienced spectators know to secure tickets in advance; hordes of walk-ups wait shivering in a line that stretches onto Seventh Avenue, where they are lashed by winter winds. It takes an hour in line to get to the box office away from the cold, but inside the Garden, it soon grows unbearably stuffy as twenty-five thousand fans, plus breeders, groomers, and handlers, crowd the floor as densely as a rush-hour subway car . . . but with the added scent each day of a thousand cooped-up dogs.

By noon the first day of the show, the suffocating conditions have begun to wilt doggie hairdos and topple weak human beings. Away from the spotlight and the arena's show rings, fatigued participants collapse in lavatories and in sawdust-strewn canine "exercise areas" where they've retreated from the mob in hopes of finding air to breathe; panting animals waiting in adjacent cages snarl at one another out of boredom and frustration. The cramped quarters are a far cry from the blue skies of the East Coast weekend when the show season started in May, but even this oppressive city air bristles with excitement. The crowds and the tumult only add to the feeling that this is the big contest, for all the marbles, comfort be damned.

To qualify for Westminster, a dog must already be an AKC champion of record, and competition is limited to 2,500 entries. If you have a champion you really want to exhibit, the most efficient way to proceed is to hire an entry service that specializes in getting dogs into shows. They make certain your entry form is delivered to the Westminster Kennel Club the moment admissions open in November. Within a few hours after that, all 2,500 places are taken and the contest is closed. Nearly every dog who makes it has been on the campaign trail all year; some have spent their lives traveling from show to show. Most all have won many breed specialties, and the really heavy hitters, resplendently advertised in a special phonebook-size edition of *Dog News,* have taken dozens of Best in Show awards. The dog favored to top the field in

1996—a high-spirited, five-year-old Afghan bitch named Tryst of Grandeur—has taken home a whopping one hundred red-white-and-blue Best in Show rosettes.

At Westminster, there are no preliminary classes as at an ordinary dog show. It is simply and dramatically a competition for Best of Breed in each of 151 breeds recognized by the American Kennel Club. In the eight felt-carpeted rings set up on the exhibition floor, judges inspect the superstars of the dog world—the finest examples of their kind on the continent—and each dog is cheered by fans who fill the box seats and bleachers and crowd around the ring. From fields that generally range from five or six specimens (only three Border Collies are entered) to thirty or forty, the judge picks one that is the best. Other than choosing Best of Breed, the judge also presents an award to the dog who is Best of Opposite Sex; and the judge is also free to select a small number of Award of Merit winners whom he or she thinks are terrific even though they didn't get the blue ribbon.

Westminster is an indoor, benched show, which means that all competing dogs—well over a thousand each day—are required to be on full display to the public in the benching area adjacent to the show rings from 11:30 A.M. to 8 P.M. Row after row of crates are packed into a long, narrow exhibition hall known as the rotunda that runs outside the ring. Here signs like those over supermarket aisles hang overhead telling which breeds are displayed where. All around this furry madhouse, concessionaires hawk dog-related toys, food, and souvenirs. There are leaden knishes to eat and vintage champagne sold by the plastic glass, doggie toenail clippers and bronze busts of Irish Wolfhounds. The man at the Fancy Publications booth yells to crowds pushing past that they can get two years of *Dog Fancy* for the price of one. At one point the mob slows to a gridlocked halt and it becomes impossible to move in any direction. Those stuck at Fancy Publications are treated to the salesman's bullhorn-loud pitch about another magazine put out by his company, this one titled *Reptiles:* "Absolutely the finest lizard magazine published in the U.S. today, bar none!"

The point of benching is to allow the public to see the dogs up close and to discuss them with exhibitors. But leisurely, thoughtful conversations are virtually impossible in the hothouse environment, which is reminiscent of an incredibly popular New York restaurant crammed with celebrities and hangers-on. Because of the claustrophobic nature of the benching area, many spectators simply stay away from the packs of people and watch the judging in the ring from the relatively comfortable seats above the action; and some exhibitors are way too busy fussing over their champions to bother talking with strangers who are bold enough to brave the mob. But most people showing dogs are here because they relish talking about what they do, so they set up makeshift displays in the limited space around their dog with portraits, business cards, photo albums of puppies they have recently produced, and leather-bound pedigrees that reveal decades of prize-winning issue. They spend hours extolling the virtues of their particular breed of dog and showing off their kennel's prize stud or bitch. And for many spectators, that is the joy of a benched show: the opportunity to hob nob with gorgeous specimens of their favorite kind of dog and with the nation's top producers of it. For those who seriously follow dog shows, being in the benching area is as thrilling as it would be for a basketball fan to be allowed to mingle with the Knicks in their locker room before a game.

Each breed is benched together, so dogs and people who are adversaries all year now stand side-by-side all day in close quarters. In general, though, camaraderie prevails: Old friends and allies from different regions compare war stories about recent show experiences and litters they have whelped, while generations of prominent bloodlines snooze behind them in their crates. The character of each cramped aisle is affected by the nature of its breed. Old English Mastiffs occupy ground that is strangely soporific despite the commotion that reigns everywhere. Many of these immense dogs, some verging on three hundred pounds, appear too big to fit comfortably in a crate, so they lounge on the floor like lazy sows, creating a snoring canine obstacle course for people trying to walk through. Smaller types of dog are elevated to eye level on grooming tables, where frantic beauticians in aprons fuss over them with combs and brushes, curling irons, hair spray, and blow-dryers. Toy Poodles, once they are prepared for the contest, are held aloft by their groomers and carried through the aisle above the heads of spectators toward the ring like precious Ming vases: their pedicured toes will touch nothing until they reach the green felt of the show ring; and God forbid anyone soil their puffy coats by petting them. A rugged-looking Bull Terrier, who would seem to require no tonsorial pyrotechnics, is deftly powdered to pristine whiteness, then a subtle line of white chalk is applied to his patent-leatherlike black nose, creating an artificial highlight that gives him a perpetual gleam.

Twenty-seven Bullmastiffs are registered for Westminster—a robust entry; they are the last breed to be judged on Monday, at four in the afternoon. Rusty—Allstar's Frisco Bay Boy—and Allstar's Mugsy Malone are benched side-by-side. At eleven in the morning, Mimi stands by their crates showing off a sheaf of snapshots of a new litter of nine puppies and telling friends of forthcoming breedings she has planned. It seems that the long Allstar puppy dry spell is coming to an end; in the next few months, there ought to be dozens of babies. Ken Vargas, who balances his own muscular bulk on a tiny folding chair, watches proudly as passers-by goo-goo at Mugsy in his crate and Mugsy returns the compliment by shooting them his most earnest Bullmastiff expression. "He's a ham!" Ken exults. "He loves being back in competition."

Debbie Vargas is not as sanguine. "This is the most repulsive show for an exhibitor and for a dog," she declares after several hours in the withering heat and jostling throngs. "They torture the dogs all day by keeping them cooped up in this airless place, just for the spectators' amusement. And yet, this is the one we all most want to win."

"I saw Mugsy Malone's name in the catalogue!" shouts one enthusiast, pushing through the Bullmastiff aisle. "Is he being shown? Is he really here?" At the sight of old Mugsy in his crate, the man stops, walks slowly forward, then drops to his knees at the wire door as if he is about to worship an incarcerated idol. He carefully scrutinizes the regal champion; and Mugsy—confounded by the man's strange behavior—gives him a piercing once-over, too. "Oh, God, he's beautiful," the man moans. "More beautiful than ever!"

Barbara Heck comes through the aisle, looking glamorous in a long fur coat. She and her husband Art have come down from Albany, fresh on the heels of their dog Sunny's Best of Breed victory at the Wallkill Kennel Club show two weeks before. Sunny (Briart's Solar Power) has been a major force in the Bullmastiff rings of the East all season, handled by Barbara herself, but surprisingly, he isn't entered in the Westminster fray. When asked why not, Barbara answers simply: "Too stressful. Not for Sunny, but for me. I couldn't stand it."

Bullmastiff fanciers begin to pack the aisle by two in the afternoon. Dr. Nakazawa, who has come to Westminster from Japan strictly as a spectator, strolls through eyeing many of the Bullmastiffs he himself judged at the breed specialty in Dallas in September. Jane Hobson, still fuming that he so cavalierly passed her and Rusty over and gave Alan Levine and his dog Thorn the top prize, announces loudly to a fellow handler: "Remember Dallas? Buddy, that's not going to happen here today!" Dr. Nakazawa smiles politely at her and moves on. "I wonder if he heard me?" Jane asks to those gathered around.

When Sherri Samel comes by, Rusty wakes from his nap and wags his tail so hard his crate shakes. He loves seeing her. She bends down and kisses him through the grate. He laps his tongue against the metal bars, trying to lick her face. "He looks good," she tells Jane with great affection for the dog that was hers for four months. Standing between him and Mugsy, Sherri gets Mimi into a close conversation to plead with her to send down another Allstar dog to work with. "Send a puppy," she says. "I'll grow him up and I'll show him. *I want to handle one of your dogs.*" Sherri, who has no Bullmastiff to show at this event—the great Mr. U's Music Man is too old, and Jane is now in charge of Rusty once again—is in competition at the Garden with a Belgian Malinois, with which she later takes Best in Breed.

"I'm in a bad spot today," says the Bullmastiff breed's greatest freelance admirer, Vito Ancona, who comes to the Garden wearing a tiny leather cap atop his gray crewcut and with the half-smoked stub of a cigarette tucked behind his ear for smoking later. "I've got too many personal friends here, too many dogs I like. I don't know who to clap for."

Despite his dilemma, it is clear that Vito has a special soft spot for Mugsy Malone. "I saw Mugsy when he was a puppy, and I have been a fan of his since the beginning. I looked at him at eight months old and I said to Mimi, *'Guaranteed winner!'* " Vito grabs Ken Vargas by the elbow and brings him into the discussion. "Kenny, what did I tell you when I saw Mugsy?"

Ken has gone through this routine before with Vito, but he doesn't at all mind playing along. Vito's familiar presence, his unbridled enthusiasm, and his occasionally mangled bons mots help dissipate the mounting anxiety of this show of shows. "Vito, you told me that this was the finest Bullmastiff you ever saw."

"That's right," Vito says. "And I said *guaranteed winner.* Didn't I, Mimi?" From across the aisle, Mimi smiles back and nods, knowing Vito is on a roll. "That Mimi!" Vito says, looking back and forth between the broad faces of Rusty and Mugsy. "If she raised iguanas, they would be the world's best iguanas." Vito reveals he is at long last getting close to making a purchase of a dog. He and Mimi have discussed the possibility of his getting a puppy from one of her future litters.

The emotional climate at the benches as people wait for the Bullmastiff judging to begin is a curious combination of tension and boredom. Vito takes off his leather cap and lays it down next to a crate, revealing a band of nervous sweat along his forehead. He fingers the cigarette butt tucked into his ear, wishing he could smoke but unwilling to leave the floor to find a smoking area. To pass time, he looks for people to whom he can hand out business cards of a new company he says he has a piece of: Charm Limousine. "That car's got everything in it," he boasts. "Soft seats, a bar, a TV, everything you'd want." But the Bullmastiff people are totally distracted by the impending contest, and few seem interested in knowing more about Vito's limos. He looks around at them, wondering aloud to himself, "Who here likes to spend any money?"

As Ken sits near Mugsy's crate on his small portable chair, wishing he had brought a cooler full of his home-brewed beer to drink, a television crew from the USA Network approaches. "We're looking for a nice-looking couple and an interesting dog," the producer says to Ken, eyeing him and Debbie and Mugsy, then calling over the on-air talent, a pretty blonde reporter dressed entirely inappropriately in pristine white slacks on which telltale dog hair and drool have already made their mark.

Ken pulls Mugsy from the crate and the big dog luxuriously stretches out on the cool floor. The reporter kneels next to him with her microphone, and as she hears Mugsy's story from the Vargases, she figures out her angle: "He's Magic Johnson!" she says. "He's making his comeback." She puts the microphone near Ken's mouth and asks, "Is Mugs nervous?"

"It's Mugsy," Ken corrects her. "And no, he isn't nervous. He loves it."

The television camera and crew make the crowd grow even denser than before. Onlookers snap pictures of the on-camera dog, some check their programs to see exactly which celebrity canine this is, some handlers grumble that *their* Bullmastiff is the one that really ought to be interviewed.

"So Mugsy is the favorite here today at the Garden?" the reporter asks, apparently unaware of Westminster's heavy favorite, the Afghan Tryst of Grandeur, or the Cocker Spaniel Bart Simpson—dogs whose incredible success make even Mugsy's show career pale by comparison.

Debbie answers diplomatically: "Well, he's the sentimental favorite, if not the oddsmakers'."

Less than an hour remains before Bullmastiff judging, and although the aisle grows increasingly crowded, it also grows quieter, as before a battle. The pressure explodes when two rival Bullmastiff fanciers face off in an argument about the moral implications of using planned cesarean sections. "Don't you point your finger at my wife!" one debater shouts at the other; and quickly the air above the swarming aisle fills with screams about uterine inertia and birth canal blockage. Fists are clenched, angry words are spat, but the combatants are held back from a knock-down fight by their allies.

In the wake of the confrontation, a silent pall hangs in the air. The tension is partially diffused when Vito Ancona steps into the center of the aisle and lets everyone around know that a friend of his who is a professional psychic to such celebrities as the late David Susskind, told him he has supernatural powers—and last night he had a vision that there would be a big fight in the Bullmastiff aisle today. To add a dramatic point to his revelation, he reaches up to snug his leather cap down over his eyes . . . but realizes it is missing—perhaps stolen. He pauses dramatically and stands center stage, his finger raised in the air with all the foreboding of a character from *Macbeth*. "Whoever took it, I wish a curse upon their head!" he pronounces.

"What's the curse? Dandruff?" someone pipes up; and blessedly, the tension breaks like a summer storm.

A few minutes before four o'clock Jane Hobson straps band number 27 onto her upper right arm, tucks a slop rag into her waistband, and leads Rusty from his crate. She wipes his back with a damp towel, bends down, glares at him nose to nose, and whispers like a trainer giving a prizefighter last-minute encouragement. As Jane leads Rusty through the crowds toward ring number 5 along with about two dozen other Bullmastiffs, Mimi allows herself one moment of hope for All-star's dogs. She has not dared imagine winning, what with Alan Levine and Thorn the odds-on favorites. But when she looks at her Rusty and at Mugsy heading toward the ring—consummate professionals, self-assured, eager to take on the world—she is overwhelmed by how good they look. How could any judge *not* see their beauty? "Oh, my, it would be nice," she says prayerfully.

Alan Levine appears ringside wearing a broad-brimmed black hat instead of his usual white straw. At the end of his lead line is Thorn, who is still far and away the top-winning

Bullmastiff in the country. Unlike the majority of Bullmastiff people, whose dogs are crated together, Levine has had Thorn benched in a separate area reserved for professionals who handle several breeds. Waiting ringside for the Great Pyrenees judging to conclude, he talks to no one; nor does he appear to work hard getting Thorn psyched up for the competition. Calm and collected, man and dog betray nothing but confidence. Arthur Einstein, Mimi's husband, has left his midtown office to come to the Garden and lend support to her cheering section. "Who's that guy?" he asks a ringside observer, pointing to Alan Levine. "He looks like he owns the place." Mimi, thankfully, does not hear his observation.

"Who's got Valium?" one handler jokes nervously as the Great Pyrenees handlers come out of the ring, bathed in sweat and looking like they've just gone fifteen rounds.

"Bring me ice!" calls another handler to an assistant when she sees her dog is panting from the heat.

"Scream and whoop for Rusty and Mugsy," Mimi reminds her allies standing ringside with her. Her focus is so complete that she hears nothing and sees only her dogs. Vito chatters on, Arthur offers words of encouragement, but Mimi's vision is focused like a laser beam on Rusty.

Judge Roy Stenmark of California calls all males into the ring first. As fourteen Bullmastiffs trot onto the green felt, applauded by contingents of their fans who crowd the ropes at the edge, Vito Ancona, still annoyed about the theft of his hat, flashes a thumbworn business card he carries from a friend who owns a hat shop. Vito, an Italian-American of the old school, is proud of his connections. "I can get another hat . . . like this!" he proclaims, snapping tobacco-stained fingers. But as the clock ticks down to final judgment, no one can even feign interest in his lost hat or the low price of its replacement.

Handler Fred Olsen gaits Mugsy Malone around the ring,

the big dog eating up the ground with the brio of a self-assured champion. "They make some team, huh, Mimi?" a bystander says; but Mimi is too focused on the action to reply. It has been a year and a half since she or anyone has seen Mugsy Malone take charge of a show ring, and it is a rousing sight. As he sails in a wide circle and the applause grows, he feeds on the admiration. By the end of one lap, he is so thrilled he leaps with joy—one hundred sixty pounds of airborne Bullmastiff, having the time of his life.

When Rusty's turn comes to show his stuff, magic happens. Despite his year's bumpy road, despite his travails from handler to handler and his uncertain future as a top-winning show dog, he charges around the ring like he owns it. He has never looked better. All the promise Mimi saw in Rusty when he was younger has reached fruition now. At the age of three, Rusty has arrived. Not as huge or as agile as Mugsy, but gloriously well-muscled, he rolls across the felt like a supercharged steamroller, his topline perfectly straight, his pink tongue wagging and a sparkle in his eyes.

Thorn, who has racked up enough points to come to the Garden as an irresistible force, gaits smooth and easy when the judge calls him out of line. He is a stately presence; and after the judge inspects all fourteen males, he points to Thorn to step out of the line. Then he points to Mugsy and Rusty and three others, signaling that these six have made his first cut. The remaining eight are excused; and with the field of males now narrowed down to six, he asks them to leave the ring so he can inspect the bitches.

In a broad waiting area outside the arena, the six handlers confer with owners and cool down their stud dogs as they wait to be called back.

"I am very pleased Rusty made the cut," Mimi says, scarcely able to hide her excitement or her nerves.

"He showed like shit," Jane says, aware of every mistake he made that no one, not even the judge, saw. "I feel like passing out. It's so hot."

"No, he moved well," Mimi says.

"That's because he's behind someone," Jane says. "He moves well when he's chasing the dog in front, but he hates it when they run up on his back."

Mimi walks over to admire Mugsy, who is cooling his stomach on the concrete floor as Ken Vargas plies apart the dog's lips and inserts a spray bottle with cold water for a few spritzes.

"The judge hardly looked at Thorn," Jane says with wonderment.

"That means one of two things," Mimi says. "Either Thorn has it made, or he's out of there."

"Thorn was breathing so hard," Ken says. "He looked so out of shape. I thought he was going to have a heart attack."

"His coat looks like someone walked all over it with golf shoes," Mimi adds. Such catty chatter is nothing new among the owners of Thorn's rivals, although it never seemed to reflect the opinion of judges, who awarded him top prizes all year long. But a current of hope still flows through the season of defeats, and it electrifies the air Mimi breathes.

To provide Rusty drinking water, Jane removes all her bait from a small cooler and offers him the icy dregs. "Liver-flavored ice water!" Jane coaxes, offering some to Mugsy, too.

Debbie Vargas drops the end of her cigarette on the concrete floor, but when she goes to stub it out she realizes she left her shoes ringside, just walked out of them in a trance when she followed Mugsy from the ring in her stocking feet.

When the top dogs are called back to join the top bitches, Mimi stands by the side of the ring holding her head as if it might otherwise explode with anxiety. From the final lineup, the judge points to Rusty, Mugsy, and Thorn. His gesture ignites cheers in Madison Square Garden. No one knows exactly what Mr. Stenmark's judging pattern is this night, but it appears he is now choosing among these three; and precedent says that the one he puts in front will be the one who wins. He puts Mugsy at the front of the line, then Rusty, then Thorn. Mimi closes her eyes and tilts her face heavenward.

The judge then turns from the three males and scrutinizes entry number 5 at the other side of the ring, Shadyoak Dox Fetching Frieda. Frieda, the top-winning Bullmastiff bitch in the country, comes from Illinois and, like Thorn, she is heavily advertised in all the major dog-show publications. But she has not been seen much in the East. She is, of course, not as imposing as the males—bitches simply aren't—but she shows with great panache and she is a dashing example of the breed, a fact even her detractors acknowledge, with one major caveat: she appears to be half the size of her male competition and considerably less than the official breed standard specifies, even for a bitch. In fact, the standard says that all other things being equal, the heavier dog should be favored. Nonetheless, Frieda comes to the Garden with the best record of any Bullmastiff other than Thorn.

"Oh, please!" Mimi spits angrily when she realizes that Judge Stenmark is actually considering Frieda, whose small size is the utter opposite of everything Allstar Kennels stands for. But he does it, he calls her out and puts her at the head of the line, asks Thorn to follow behind her, then tells the foursome—Frieda, Thorn, Mugsy, and Rusty—to gait around the ring. "Wrong order, wrong order!" Mugsy's fans shout, knowing full well what is about to happen. One half-circle around the ring and Stenmark points to Frieda as number one and to Thorn as Best of Opposite Sex. Mugsy and Rusty win Awards of Merit.

"They gave the ribbon to a Rhodesian Ridgeback!" Vito Ancona pronounces cynically as Frieda takes her victory lap. "What a waste of time. And for this, I had to lose a hat!"

An Award of Merit at Westminster is not a Best of Breed rosette, but in the world of show dogs, it ain't chopped liver. The fact is, the veteran Mugsy and newcomer Rusty showed beautifully, and to have produced two dogs in the top four is a fine achievement for any kennel. When the formal photograph is taken of Rusty with his prize, Jane holds his leash and Mimi stands off camera, baiting her boy and smiling at him and Jane with tremendous pride. He did well; Jane did well; Allstar looked terrific in the ring.

Even if she didn't win the big one, Mimi feels reborn. The torments of breeding, the sick puppies, all the fights and rivalries and petty annoyances of the show ring have been, for now, wiped away. Rusty did better than she thought he would; she announces that Jane will be campaigning him again this year. And he will be joined by Allstar's Sonny Boy—Sam's progeny—who will make his ring debut at the East Coast Weekend in May, also handled by Jane Hobson.

Monday night, the first of the two-day show, is when all the best working dogs go into the ring to compete for Best of Group. Frieda the Bullmastiff holds little interest for the judge, Mrs. J. A. Goodin, who selects a California Boxer nicknamed Future as best of all the working dogs. So with no Bullmastiff left in the contest, Mimi stays home Tuesday and watches the Best in Show finale on television at home. She and her husband Arthur and friends sit in the family room drinking champagne and eating chocolate mousse cake, as twelve-week-old Sophie—the solitary puppy from Blossom's lonely litter—cuddles with them on the couch and the climactic events at Westminster are broadcast.

Allstar's Play It Again Sam, in whom Mimi had placed so

much hope at the beginning of the season but who has now retired to a happy life of making babies and being a house dog, lounges on his own personal ottoman by a crackling fire beneath the television. "Sam is going to be a grandfather," Mimi says, informing her guests that his son Sonny—who looks like he could become a great show dog to reckon with this year—was bred for the first time earlier in the day to a bitch from Pennsylvania. Sam, snoozing comfortably without a care in the world, is indifferent to grandfatherhood; and he scarcely looks up at the television when the crowd roars as Tryst of Grandeur, the stupendously showy Afghan Hound, sails around the ring in Best in Show competition. To the surprise of everyone who follows dog shows, Tryst does not take Best in Show. She is defeated by the most unlikely of dark horses, a Clumber Spaniel named Clussexx Country Sunrise. Clumbers are a lot like Bullmastiffs: big and lovably ungainly, a breed with no particular popularity or fame. In Mimi's eyes, and in the eyes of breeders around the country, the Clumber's upset win is a sign from above. There is always hope for victory, and the next show down the road could be where it's going to happen.

Where Are They Now?

RUSTY

After Rusty's fine showing at Westminster, Mimi buys the deluxe dog treadmill for Jane Hobson, who takes Rusty on it for a workout almost every day. His physical maturity and his show ring experience, combined with his new exercise regime, have made him one of the top-ten Bullmastiffs in the nation and number one in the northeast.

SAM

In the spring, puppies chewed the corners off his favorite ottoman, which has been reupholstered. Mimi estimates he has sired fifty puppies, so far.

SUGAR

Spayed and living in White Plains, New York, Sugar has found a new home without any other dogs or children, where life centers entirely around her.

SONNY BOY

All the formerly exasperating puppy exuberance of this son of Sam has translated into an ebullient and irresistable show ring personality. Sonny earns his championship in six outings, including an amazing four majors; at less than two years old, he will join Rusty in the ring of champions at the Westminster Kennel Club show in 1997.

SOPHIE

Blossom Dearie's last puppy, sired by Mugsy Malone, begins her show career at the Bullmastiff specialty show in Greenwich in June, 1996. "She is dynamite," Mimi says. "She will be a superstar in the show ring. At home, she is not exactly working her way into Doris's shoes—because those cannot be filled—but she is going to be *my* dog."

MUGSY MALONE

After his Award of Merit at Westminster, Mugsy moved to Chicago with his owners Ken and Debbie Vargas. Debbie reports, "Indoors, he is basically the same old couch potato, but outside he is making lots of new friends. Three young children who live next door throw sticks for him to retrieve, and on the other side of us there is a Scottish Deerhound he likes very much." The hound is a male, but there's no growling machismo in this situation. "Mugsy is a different dog at home than he is at shows. Here at home, he gets along well with everyone and almost every dog—female or male— which is a lot different than at dog shows, where he has an ego that is way too big for his already big head and has to prove that he's top dog."

BILL AND BONNIE WILSON

Aspen vom Birkenwald, the puppy kept by the Wilsons from their breeding of Koko to Jabba, won Best of Winners at the 1996 Leonberger Specialty show. They acquired a young bitch from England—Manorguard's Guiding Star—in hopes of breeding her to Aspen, but at the age of six months she is beginning to look like she will not grow large enough to make a good match. If she turns out to be unsuitably small for breeding, the Wilsons plan to test her talents at obedience work. Meanwhile, another breeding is planned for Koko, using frozen sperm from an Italian Leonberger champion named Zelda's Foxtrot.

LADYBUG THORN OF THE ROSE B.D.

After taking a Best of Opposite Sex award at Westminster in 1996, the five-year-old champion went into what his handler, Alan Levine, calls "semiretirement"—just a few local shows, but no major campaign as in previous years. Of the top-winning Bullmastiff of 1995, Levine says, "Thorn has done his part, he fought a good fight."

ALAN LEVINE

The man who took Thorn to the summit of glory is now handling Lookout's Locomotion, the puppy who won the Junior

Dog class at the 1995 Bullmastiff specialty—a combination of dog and handler that Mimi Einstein then feared could be "unstoppable." Levine predicts, "When he fills out, he will be the dog to beat."

VITO ANCONA

On Thursday, May 23, 1996, Vito Ancona finally found the Bullmastiff of his dreams. He arrived at Mimi's house in the morning with a bag full of Italian pastries, and after coffee and cannoli, he went into a grassy fenced-in yard with three lovely red puppies—two girls and a boy. He lay on the grass to see which of the three was friendliest and licked his face the most. Finally, he announced, "This is like shooting crap," and selected the bitch with the slightly bigger head.

He may have taken the better part of a decade to make up his mind to actually buy a dog, but there was one thing of which Vito Ancona was absolutely certain. This new puppy of his would be treated like royalty. If she develops into a beautiful show ring prospect, the sky's the limit. "Daddy will support you in the Miss America contest," he tells the eight-week-old, "but if you turn into Gravel Gertie, that's okay, too. You can get a very good job in nursing."

Before leaving, Vito explained his theory of puppy training: "For the first six months, it is absolutely important that she not be exposed to any yelling or chaos or confusion. Just quiet and love, from everyone around her. No matter what she does, she will not be scolded and no one will ever hurt her. This is a breed that never forgets—good things and bad things—and she is going to learn to think only good thoughts when she thinks of me. Do you know the main difference between humans and dogs? Dogs see their God every day."

Basic Show Dog Terms

Words and phrases frequently heard around the ring and kennel

angulation: the flow of a dog's leg joints

bitchy: a male dog that looks like a female

blocky: a squarish shape, usually referring to the head

bossy: overmuscled shoulders

bracelets: the fur puffs on a poodle's legs

brindle: a tweedlike coat of tan with black marbling

brisket: the front part of a dog's chest

by: parented by (referring to the sire, or father)

camel-backed: a top line that curves upward in the middle

cat-footed: toes held close together

chalked: a coat that has been artificially colored

cheeky: large-jowled

chisled: buffed, meaning the musculature is apparent

close-coupled: short-backed

cobby: a compact appearance

corky: exuberant and alert

correction: a sharp yank on the collar by a handler to get a dog's full attention

cow-hocked: back feet turn outward

crabby: moves on a slant, rather than on a straight line

dewlaps: flaps that hang from the throat of loose-skinned dogs

dish-faced: with a concave muzzle

doggy: a female dog that looks like a male

domed: round-skulled

Basic Show Dog Terms

down-faced: with a convex muzzle
dudley: flesh-colored nose
east-west: splay-footed
fiddle-faced: a long, narrow face
fiddle-fronted: bow-legged
finish: attain championship
flat-sided: ribs not rounded enough; also *slab-sided*
flews: the long, droopy part of the lips on loose-skinned dogs
gay-tailed: tail carried high and over the back
get: offspring
hare-footed: with a long, narrow foot
harlequin: white with black markings
issue: offspring
major: a show in which three or more points can be earned
off: lame
out of: parented by (referring to the dam, or mother)
overdone: too typey
poky: head carried too far forward
put down: impeccably groomed
rangy: long-bodied
roach-backed: a curve in the lower back
slew-footed: a foot that turns outward
snipey: pointy-muzzled
sound: physically fit (not lame)
special: a special is a dog entered in a show who is already a champion
spectacled: darkly marked around the eyes
springy: well-rounded in the ribs
stack: to stand a dog at attention for scrutiny by a judge
standard: the written description of a breed, prescribing perfection
throaty: loose-skinned around the neck
tucked up: thin-waisted
typey: showing the breed characteristics to maximum effect
weedy: delicate
wry: crooked-jawed

Breeds Recognized by the AKC

SPORTING DOGS

Brittanys

Pointers

German Short-haired Pointers

German Wire-haired Pointers

Chesapeake Bay Retrievers

Curly-Coated Retrievers

Flat-Coated Retrievers

Golden Retrievers

Labrador Retrievers

English Setters

Gordon Setters

Irish Setters

American Water Spaniels

Clumber Spaniels

Black Cocker Spaniels

Ascob Cocker Spaniels

Parti-Color Cocker Spaniels

English Cocker Spaniels

English Springer Spaniels

Field Spaniels

Irish Water Spaniels

Sussex Spaniels

Welsh Springer Spaniels

Vizslas

Weimaraners

Wire-haired Pointing Griffons

Breeds Recognized by the AKC

HOUND DOGS

Afghan Hounds
Basenjis
Basset Hounds
Thirteen-Inch Beagles
Fifteen-Inch Beagles
Black and Tan Coonhounds
Bloodhounds
Borzois
Long-haired Dachshunds
Smooth Dachshunds
Wire-haired Dachshunds
American Foxhounds
English Foxhounds

Greyhounds
Harriers
Ibizan Hounds
Irish Wolfhounds
Norwegian Elkhounds
Otterhounds
Petits Bassets Griffons Vendeens
Pharaoh Hounds
Rhodesian Ridgebacks
Salukis
Scottish Deerhounds
Whippets

WORKING DOGS

Akitas
Alaskan Malamutes
Bernese Mountain dogs
Boxers
Bullmastiffs
Doberman Pinschers
Giant Schnauzers
Great Danes
Great Pyrenees
Greater Swiss Mountain dogs

Komondoroks
Kuvaszoks
Mastiffs
Newfoundlands
Portuguese Water dogs
Rottweilers
Saint Bernards
Samoyeds
Siberian Huskies
Standard Schnauzers

Breeds Recognized by the AKC

TERRIER DOGS

Airedale Terriers

American Staffordshire Terriers

Australian Terriers

Bedlington Terriers

Border Terriers

Colored Bull Terriers

White Bull Terriers

Cairn Terriers

Dandie Dinmont Terriers

Smooth Fox Terriers

Wire Fox Terriers

Irish Terriers

Kerry Blue Terriers

Lakeland Terriers

Standard Manchester Terriers

Miniature Bull Terriers

Miniature Schnauzers

Norfolk Terriers

Norwich Terriers

Scottish Terriers

Sealyham Terriers

Skye Terriers

Soft-Coated Wheaton Terriers

Staffordshire Bull Terriers

Welsh Terriers

West Highland White Terriers

TOY DOGS

Affenpinschers

Brussels Griffons

Cavalier King Charles Spaniels

Long Coat Chihuahuas

Smooth Coat Chihuahuas

Chinese Crested dogs

Blenheim & Prince Charles
    English Toy Spaniels

King Charles and Ruby
    English Toy Spaniels

Italian Greyhounds

Japanese Chins

Maltese

Toy Manchester Terriers

Miniature Pinschers

Papillons

Pekingese

Pomeranians

Toy Poodles

Pugs

Shih Tzus

Silky Terriers

Yorkshire Terriers

Breeds Recognized by the AKC

Non-Sporting Dogs

American Eskimo dogs

Bichons Frises

Boston Terriers

Bulldogs

Chinese Shar-Peis

Chow Chows

Dalmatians

Finnish Spitzes

French Bulldogs

Keeshonden

Lhasa Apsos

Miniature Poodles

Standard Poodles

Schipperkes

Shiba Inus

Tibetan Spaniels

Tibetan Terriers

Herding Dogs

Australian Cattle dogs

Australian Shepherds

Bearded Collies

Belgian Malinois

Belgian Sheepdogs

Belgian Tervurens

Border Collies

Bouviers des Flandres

Briards

Rough Collies

Smooth Collies

German Shepherd dogs

Old English Sheepdogs

Puliks

Shetland Sheepdogs

Cardigan Welsh Corgis

Pembroke Welsh Corgis

APPENDIX 3

The Most Popular Breeds

The rise of the Rottweiler to the second-most popular dog in America (from number 15 in 1986) and the sudden appearance of the Shar-Pei among the Top Ten are two of the big stories told by the following statistics, which represent the number of each breed registered with the American Kennel Club during the calendar year. In fact, the Shar-Pei figures are skewed by the fact that 1992 was the first year the breed was recognized by the AKC, so the number of registrations reflects not only new puppies but also all the known foundation stock. In 1995, Shar-Peis were actually twenty-seventh most popular among all breeds registered by the AKC.

Bullmastiffs, by the way, rated sixty-seventh in 1986, fifty-third in 1995.

To give some idea of what these rankings mean, there were 132,000 Labrador Retrievers registered in 1995, 94,000 Rottweilers, 78,000 German Shepherd dogs, 13,000 Shar-Peis, and 2,575 Bullmastiffs.

The least-registered AKC breed over the last decade has consistently been the Harrier: a total of 129 dogs in 1986, 140 in 1995. Harriers are an ancient breed, their forefathers going back at least to the thirteenth century, when hares were considered good food in England and they were hunted by men on foot (rather than ahorse), accompanied by packs of their eager little hare-hounds.

THE MOST POPULAR BREEDS

1986

1. Cocker Spaniels
2. Poodles
3. Labrador Retrievers
4. Golden Retrievers
5. German Shepherd dogs
6. Chow Chows
7. Beagles
8. Miniature Schnauzers
9. Dachshunds
10. Shetland Sheepdogs

1988

1. Cocker Spaniels
2. Labrador Retrievers
3. Poodles
4. Golden Retrievers
5. German Shepherd dogs
6. Chow Chows
7. Rottweilers
8. Beagles
9. Dachshunds
10. Miniature Schnauzers

1990

1. Cocker Spaniels
2. Labrador Retrievers
3. Poodles
4. Golden Retrievers
5. Rottweilers
6. German Shepherd dogs
7. Chow Chows
8. Dachshunds
9. Beagles
10. Miniature Schnauzers

1992

1. Labrador Retrievers
2. Rottweilers
3. Cocker Spaniels
4. Chinese Shar-Peis
5. German Shepherd dogs
6. Poodles
7. Golden Retrievers
8. Beagles
9. Dachshunds
10. Shetland Sheepdogs

1994

1. Labrador Retrievers
2. Rottweilers
3. German Shepherd dogs
4. Golden Retrievers
5. Poodles
6. Cocker Spaniels
7. Beagles
8. Dachshunds
9. Dalmatians
10. Pomeranians

1995

1. Labrador Retrievers
2. Rottweilers
3. German Shepherd dogs
4. Golden Retrievers
5. Beagles
6. Poodles
7. Cocker Spaniels
8. Dachshunds
9. Pomeranians
10. Yorkshire Terriers